Psychological Warfare in Business:

THE RULES THEY NEVER TOLD YOU

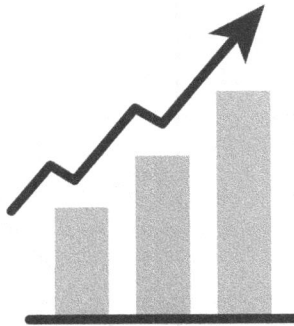

LARRY JAY LEVINE

Psychological Warfare in Business: The Rules They Never Told You

Copyright © 2025 Larry Jay Levine
All rights reserved.

This book is a work of nonfiction based on the author's opinions, research, and personal experiences within the federal prison system. It is intended for informational purposes only and should not be construed as legal advice or a guaranteed strategy for navigating incarceration. While the author and publisher have made every effort to ensure the accuracy and completeness of the information presented, they disclaim all liability for any errors, omissions, or outcomes resulting from the use of this book.

Legal Disclaimer:

The author and publisher are not lawyers. The strategies, insights, and opinions presented in this book are for informational purposes only and are not a substitute for professional legal advice. Readers are strongly advised to consult a licensed attorney for any legal concerns or questions related to their specific circumstances. By using the information in this book, you agree that the author and publisher will not be held liable for any outcomes resulting from its application.

First Edition

Printed in the United States of America

Publisher Information:

World Crime Media Inc
Sheridan, Wyoming
For inquiries contact **help@worldcrimemedia.com**

ISBN: *979-8-9940198-0-1*

Additional Notes:

All names, dates, and specific details in any examples or case studies presented have been altered to protect the identities of those involved. Any resemblance to actual persons, living or dead, is purely coincidental unless otherwise stated.

Terms of Use:

Disclaimer

This book isn't written for the fragile, the fake-motivated, or the self-help junkies who can't handle a little truth without a trigger warning. It's written for people who want to understand how psychological warfare actually works — in business, politics, relationships, or any other human battlefield where control and influence decide who eats and who gets eaten.

Everything you're about to read is based on real tactics, real behavioral science, and real-world observation. None of it is fantasy. But don't twist that into permission to go start your own personal coup. The material here is for **education, defense, and awareness**, not for breaking laws, ruining lives, or playing amateur puppet master with people who don't deserve it. If you weaponize this information and end up on the evening news, that's on you, not me.

Let's make this perfectly clear: **nothing** in these pages is professional advice. I'm not your lawyer, therapist, or moral compass. If you've got an impulse to go full-villain with what you learn, call a shrink or an attorney before you act, because you won't be blaming this book for your bad decisions later.

The examples, stories, and scenarios are a mix of reality, sarcasm, and metaphor — designed to punch through the noise and show how manipulation actually functions. Some details have been altered for privacy, security, or dramatic clarity, but the principles remain sharp enough to cut.

This is a field manual for thinkers — not criminals, cult leaders, or the perpetually offended. Use what's inside to protect yourself, to understand power when it's being used against you, and to recognize how easy it is to be controlled without ever realizing it. If you're smart, it'll wake you up. If you're reckless, it'll burn you.

Read at your own risk. Learn at your own speed. And remember: **Knowledge is power — but misuse it, and power becomes a weapon you turn on yourself.**

Preface

If you picked this book up because you like feel-good slogans, motivational wallpaper, or someone telling you to "just be yourself," put it down now and save us both the headache. This isn't a pep talk. This isn't a therapy session. This is a field manual — ugly, practical, and true — about how people take power, keep power, and bend other people's choices without the other person noticing until it's too late.

I've spent my life watching the game from inside and outside the ring. I've seen how smart people drown in their own politeness, how institutions hide brutality behind procedure, and how "nice" can be a tactical weakness. I've watched careers die because someone didn't understand a three-sentence framing move. I've watched empires shift because one person learned how to control the story. None of this is theoretical. It's lived, observed, stolen, and reverse-engineered.

Why write this book? Because the world already teaches manipulation — you just get it in classes framed as manners, marketing, or law. I want to rip the purple curtain off and show you the machinery. Not to glamorize cruelty, but to arm you. To make you harder to fuck with. To show you how to spot the quiet tactics that rob you of autonomy one polite concession at a time. If you read this and decide to go become a monster, that's on you. If you read this and become harder to manipulate, safer in boardrooms and bedrooms, and smarter about the narratives being piled on you — mission accomplished.

How to use this book:
 Read like you mean it. This isn't material you skim between tweets. Each chapter is a tool chest. Some of the tools are blunt;

some are delicate. Practice the ones that fit your needs and your ethics. You don't have to become a sociopath to survive in hostile systems — but you do need to know their rules, their vulnerabilities, and their lies.

Expect three things on every page:

First, clarity — I'll break down the tactic, why it works, and where it shows up. Second, examples — stories, case studies, and yes, a little theatrical cruelty to make the lesson stick. Third, a hard look at consequences — what happens if you use it, or if it's used on you. No hand-holding. No moral pretense. Just a relentless map of how influence actually operates.

You'll also notice the voice: sarcastic, unpolished, and loud. That's deliberate. Language is part of the attack and the defense. Tone frames reality. If a sentence doesn't hit, rewrite it. If an idea doesn't make you flinch, it isn't sharp enough. I write like I fight: quick, ruthless, and to the point.

A few honest boundaries:

This book does not teach you how to commit crimes, stalk, or harass. If you're looking for a blueprint to break the law or ruin people, don't pretend this gave you permission — you chose that path. I'm not your lawyer, your counselor, or your moral guide. If you're about to do something risky, talk to a professional who actually takes responsibility for outcomes. What I give you is knowledge. How you use it is your problem.

Also: context matters. A tactic that's lethal in a corporate meeting might be useless or destructive in a marriage. Learn to adapt. Learn to calibrate. Weaponize only what you can control and only when you've calculated the fallout. Sometimes the best move is to walk away.

What you'll walk away with:

- A vocabulary for the invisible forces that shape decisions.

- A toolkit to spot manipulation from the cheap and the sophisticated.

- Tactics you can use to protect yourself, make better calls, and win when it counts.

- A sharper bullshit detector — priceless, and often underpriced.

If you want to be pretty and popular, this book will make you dangerous instead. That's the point. The world doesn't reward politeness; it rewards outcomes. Learn to get the outcomes you want without losing your soul. Or don't. But if you're reading this, I'm betting you already know why you need it.

One last thing: power is mundane. It's paperwork and tone and timing. It's not always dramatic. Most of the time it's tiny moves repeated until they become fate. That's where the real victories are won and lost. Learn the small things, and the big things follow.

Psychological Warfare in Business:
The Rules They Never Told You

Hi I'm Larry Jay Levine your new favorite author, and before we talk tactics, let me be clear: I didn't learn this shit in a business school classroom. I learned it in the real world—the kind of world where contracts get shredded behind closed doors, where loyalty is a weapon, and where smiles are sharper than knives. I've been in backrooms where the deal was already decided before the first handshake. I've watched cowards climb ladders by stepping on people they called "partners." And I've studied, weaponized, and deployed psychological warfare not just to survive—but to dominate.

I've been trained in the kind of manipulation that makes HR departments piss themselves. This book isn't hypothetical. It's not theory. It's field-tested strategy for people who are sick of watching the clueless win while the competent get steamrolled. You want polite? Buy a Hallmark card. You want power? Turn the fucking page.

If you're looking for feel-good fluff, self-help affirmations, or corporate HR-approved bullshit, slam this book shut and walk away. Right now. No seriously—get the hell out. This book isn't safe. It's not kind. And it sure as shit isn't here to coddle your delicate sense of professional optimism.

This is not a book for the "let's circle back" crowd. This is a weapon—disguised as pages. It's built to unmask the sociopaths in corner offices, expose the manipulative charmers on sales calls, and equip you with psychological ammunition to outmaneuver, outclass, and out-control everyone who ever made you feel like you were playing catch-up.

Inside these chapters, we don't sugar-coat. We name names— like manipulation, emotional leverage, gaslighting, silence as a power play, and perception as currency. If those words scare you, you're not ready to win. Because while you were obsessing over LinkedIn endorsements, someone else was learning how to fake empathy, hijack your confidence, and out-talk you in every boardroom you walked into.

And yes, we swear. A lot. Not because it's edgy. Because it's honest. And because no one ever took over a company or shut down a power play by whispering politely. If profanity offends you more than deception, you're not the reader this book is for. But if you're the one who sees the bullshit, smells the power games, and wants to stop playing defense and start going on the attack—

Let's Be Clear: This Is a Playbook, Not a Pep Talk

Forget everything you think you know about business books. This isn't your CEO's favorite leadership memoir. This isn't a case study from Harvard. And it damn sure isn't a repackaged TED Talk about resilience or "authenticity."

This book is a battlefield manual. A psychological dissection of how people actually behave when money, status, ego, and survival are on the line. It doesn't tell you how to be a better person—it shows you how to win, even when the deck is stacked and the rules are written in invisible ink.

We break business down to its rawest components: - Perception - Control - Leverage - Obedience - Influence - Psychological warfare disguised as meetings, contracts, performance reviews, and coffee chats

Each section dives deep into the anatomy of power. You'll get labeled lessons, broken down into specific tactics. We don't talk in theory—we talk in weapon systems. And every single tactic has been field-tested in real-world business scenarios, from boardrooms to break rooms, mergers to meltdowns.

You're not getting advice. You're getting a goddamn blueprint. And yeah, it's ruthless. But so is business. So is the asshole who took credit for your work. So is the client who ghosted after you bent over backwards. So is the boss who kept promoting idiots because they "played the game."

Don't Just Read This. Weaponize It

This isn't a book you read once and shelve like a motivational poster. This is an operating manual for people who intend to win. Not just occasionally. Always. Use this book like an assassin uses a blade. Quietly. Strategically. Without warning. These pages are not for display—they're for deployment.

Each chapter is a psychological war zone. Every lesson, a deconstructed power play. Every tactic, a grenade with the pin already half-pulled. Your job isn't to admire them—it's to use them. If you're in sales, this book will teach you how to get them to beg for the deal. If you're in management, it'll show you how to own a room without saying a word. If you're just starting out, this book is the fastest shortcut to seeing how the power grid of any organization really works—and where the weaknesses live.

And if you're already seasoned? This will sharpen every edge you've dulled by playing nice for too long. Read it front to back, or skip to the chapters that speak to your situation. Highlight, annotate, abuse the pages. Read it once and then again with someone else's behavior in mind. Then read it a third time, but this time with your own fingerprints all over it—so you can see where you've been played, and where you need to strike next.

You'll never walk into a meeting blind again. You'll never get caught off guard. You'll never be the pawn pretending to be the king. Because once this knowledge is in your head, it never leaves. And neither does the power that comes with it.

Dedication

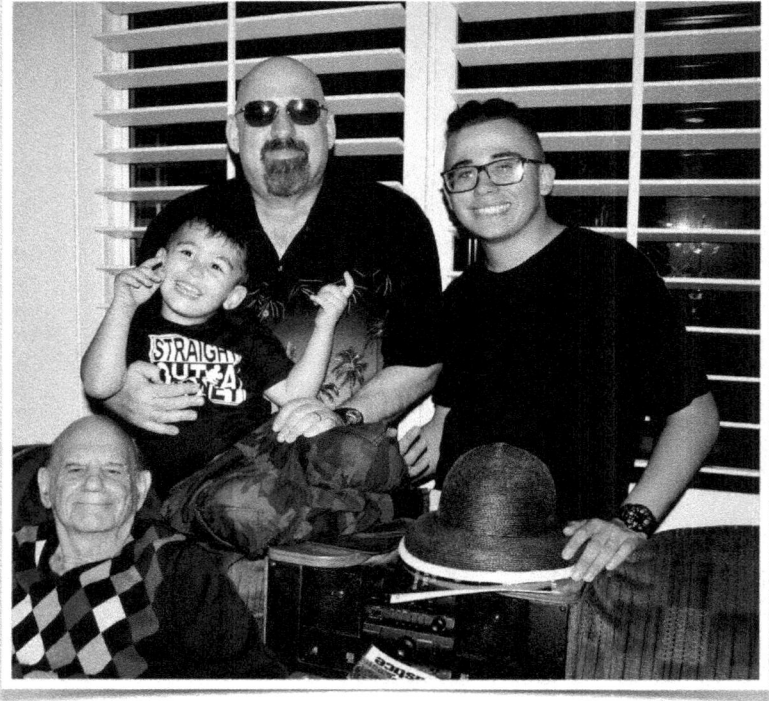

To my father, **Ron Levine**, — a child of the Depression, a brilliant businessman, a hell of an investor, and one of the most hard-headed, opinionated men to ever walk the earth. He isn't warm, he isn't fuzzy, but he's sharp. He understands people, money, and pressure better than anyone I've ever met. A lot of what I know about reading the world came from watching him. His health might be failing, but that stubborn fire in him never did.

To my grandsons, **Jojo** and **Lucas** — two genuinely good kids who somehow dodged most of the family attitude.

Jojo, you went into caregiving and psychology of sorts, which is impressive, because I don't know how you deal with that many emotions without throwing someone out a window. You've got more patience than I ever will, and you see people from angles most folks never do.

Lucas, you're the scientist in the making — curious, quick, and wired to figure out how everything works. Just don't dissect anything alive in the kitchen and we'll call it a win.

You both need to do what makes you happy and live your life for yourselves. You're going to disagree with people, and people are going to disagree with you — that's just how life works. Just because you, I, or anyone else believes something doesn't make it true. People will deceive you and mislead you for reasons you'll never fully understand. And you'll learn that sometimes it's better to say nothing at all while quietly knowing the truth. That's where strength — and real control — begins.

And me?
 This book isn't some emotional family heirloom. It's a field guide built from the mistakes I made, the things I've seen, the shit I survived, and the people I learned to read the hard way. If any part of this helps you cut through bullshit faster, think sharper, or dodge a few of the traps life throws at you, then that's worth more than any sentimental legacy I could pretend to leave.

Different generations. Different worlds.
 Same blood — and hopefully, fewer dumb decisions.

-"Vincit qui se vincit."

My Daily Writing Companion Hazel

"Crazy Hazy" is a purebred purple tongue Chow Chow that my wife Letecia and I rescued when she was a puppy just before Covid. If she's not busying playing or destroying her toys, she's constantly busting my balls banging on the door demanding to be let in or out, and can be found nearby as I write, trying to charm more nummies from me!

TABLE OF CONTENTS

Chapter One: The Mechanics of Power and Control

Power isn't given—it's taken, twisted, and welded into your identity. This chapter breaks down how control actually works: perception, suggestion, dominance, and emotional leverage. You'll learn how to become the force that shapes conversations, moods, and decisions without ever asking for permission. Power's not a title—it's a tactic. And after this chapter, you'll never see it as optional again.

Lesson One:

- **Tactic 1.1:** What Power Really Is (And Isn't) – Perception Is King

- **Tactic 1.2:** The Confidence Conspiracy – Swagger Runs the World

- **Tactic 1.3:** The Illusion of Authority – Costumes Make Kings

- **Tactic 1.4:** Why the Powerful Never Explain Themselves

Lesson Two:

- **Tactic 2.1:** The Emotion Hack – Logic Doesn't Win Shit

- **Tactic 2.2:** The Familiarity Trap – Repeat the Lie Until It's Gospel

- **Tactic 2.3:** The Charisma Effect – Facts Don't Win, Vibes Do

- **Tactic 2.4:** How to Make People Rely on You Without Realizing It

Chapter Two: Exploiting Psychological Weaknesses 22

Most people are emotional landmines waiting to be stepped on— and this chapter hands you the map. Learn to spot the cracks, predict the breakdowns, and manipulate every soft spot for your own gain. You'll use their trauma, habits, and blind spots to build your own throne. This isn't empathy. This is war—and you're going to start winning it with their own emotions as your weapons.

Lesson Five:

- ⊚ **Tactic 5.1:** Conversational Manipulation: How to Set Traps & Keep People Chasing You

- ⊚ **Tactic 5.2:** Using Small Wins to Build Massive Control Over Time

- ⊚ **Tactic 5.3:** The Confusion Strategy – How to Spot, Exploit, and Keep People Off-Balance

- ⊚ **Tactic 5.4:** The Dependency Cycle – How Emotional Chaos and Control Keep People Hooked

Chapter Three: The Puppet Master's Playbook *54*

Real control doesn't shout—it whispers, edits, and deletes. This chapter shows you how to shape reality itself through framing, omission, misdirection, and fake transparency. You'll learn how to lie without lying and how to manipulate truth like a sculptor with clay. The best manipulators aren't obvious—they're the ones writing the script while everyone else thinks it's a documentary.

Lesson Six:

- ⊚ **Tactic 6.1:** The Psychology Behind Gaslighting – Why It Works

- ⊚ **Tactic 6.2:** Gaslighting in Action – Real-World Tactics to Make Them Question Everything

- ⊚ **Tactic 6.3:** Controlling the Narrative Through Framing and Omission

- ⊚ **Tactic 6.4:** How to Make Your Version of Events the 'Official' Version

Chapter Four: Subliminal Psychological Warfare 83

If you think you have to speak to control someone, you've already missed the point. This chapter dives into sensory sabotage, environmental manipulation, reflex control, and emotional conditioning. You'll turn rooms into traps, moments into programming, and people into Pavlovian pets without them ever knowing. Influence becomes instinct when the battlefield is their subconscious—and this chapter shows you how to own it.

Confidence isn't self-esteem—it's a weapon. This chapter rips apart the myths and rebuilds you as a presence that dominates space without trying. Silence, eye contact, indifference, scarcity, and surgical assertiveness become your new toolkit. You don't need to speak louder—you need to matter more. This is about making people chase you, fear losing you, and worship your approval like it's oxygen

- ◉ **Tactic 12.1:** How to Walk, Talk, and Overpower Without Saying a Damn Word

- ◉ **Tactic 12.2:** The "No Hesitation" Rule – Why Certainty Creates Power

- ◉ **Tactic 12.3:** The Dominance Effect – Make Yourself Big, Make Them Feel Tiny

- ◉ **Tactic 12.4:** Using Strategic Eye Contact to Force Submission

- ◉ **Tactic 13.1:** Commanding Respect with Silence and Sound

- ◉ **Tactic 13.2:** How to Subtly Cut Off People Who Talk Too Much

- ◉ **Tactic 13.3:** Indifference & Scarcity – The Art of Making People Chase

- ◉ **Tactic 13.4:** How to Make People Invest in You Emotionally

Negotiation is psychological warfare with a smile. You'll learn to bait, trap, and bleed them dry while making them think it was their idea. This chapter is about fake scarcity, pre-win dominance, emotional leverage, and timing that breaks wills. Forget "finding the middle ground." You're here to own the battlefield, set the terms, and walk away with everything while they thank you for it.

- **Tactic 14.1:** Controlling Opening Gambits – Why You Let Them Go First & Never Take the First Offer

- **Tactic 14.2:** Framing the Deal – Control Expectations, Feed Their Ego, Take It All

- **Tactic 14.3:** Creating Urgency – Using Scarcity and Deadlines to Force Quick Deals

- **Tactic 15.1:** The Psychological Chokehold – Weaponizing Time & Silence

- **Tactic 15.2:** Pre-Win Dominance – How to Make Them Sell Themselves to You

- **Tactic 15.3:** Emotional Triggers & Fear Tactics – Breaking Them Without Saying a Word

- **Tactic 15.4:** The Power of Walking Away – How Small Losses Win Big Wars=

- **Tactic 15.5:** Creating Dependency – How to Build Long-Term Influence They Can't Escape

Power isn't loud—it's engineered silence, manufactured chaos, and emotional sabotage dressed in leadership. This chapter teaches you to create fear-based obedience, weaponize trust, and dominate without ever raising your voice. You'll master the art of invisible control—where people follow not because you told them to, but because they're too scared or confused to do anything else.

Lesson Eighteen:

- **Tactic 18.1:** The Power of Indifference – Why Not Giving a Shit Is a Superpower

- **Tactic 18.2:** Preemptive Strikes – Hit First, Ask Questions Never

- **Tactic 18.3:** The Predator's Mindset – Never Think Like Prey

Chapter Eight: Managing the Fallout

When your manipulation gets exposed, the amateurs panic. This chapter shows you how to rebuild, redirect, and control the damage like it was part of the plan all along. Sympathy, blame shifting, fake apologies, and silent rebranding become your playbook. The goal isn't to avoid getting caught—it's to make them regret ever doubting you. Every setback becomes a setup for your next power move.

Lesson Nineteen:

- **Tactic 19.1:** The First Rule of Damage Control – Stay Calm, Stay Strategic

- **Tactic 19.2:** Weaponizing Sympathy – How to Turn the Attack on Them

- **Tactic 19.3:** Destroying Their Credibility Without Leaving Fingerprints

Lesson Twenty:

- **Tactic 20.1:** The Silent Rebuild – How to Regain Control After a Setback

- **Tactic 20.2:** The "Fake Apology" Trick – Saying Sorry Without Admitting Guilt

- **Tactic 20.3:** The Blame Shift Game – How to Make Someone Else the Fall Guy

Lesson Twenty-One:

- **Tactic 21.1:** Why Silence Can Be the Most Powerful Response

- **Tactic 21.2:** The Art of the Slow Narrative Shift – Turning an Enemy Into a Fool Over Time

- **Tactic 21.3:** How to Rebuild Your Image After a Public Hit

- **Tactic 21.4:** Turning Your Setbacks Into Power Moves

- **Tactic 21.5:** Never Let Them See You Weaken

Chapter Nine: The Psychology of Legacy *211*

This isn't about winning today. It's about never having to fight again. Legacy is the art of becoming irreplaceable, embedding yourself into systems, and owning the future by manipulating the present. This chapter shows you how to make people need you long after you're gone. Influence becomes infrastructure. Power becomes permanent. And when you get there—no one can take you out.

Lesson Twenty-Two:

- **Tactic 22.1:** Why Power is a Long Game – Thinking 10 Moves Ahead

- **Tactic 22.2:** The Immortal Influence – Staying Relevant Even After You Step Back

CHAPTER ONE

The Mechanics of Power and Control

They don't hand out power. You take it. And in this game, showing strength matters more than having it. This chapter blows apart the delusion that power is earned by talent or honesty. Spoiler: it's not. It's performed. Controlled. Rehearsed like a play and sold like a scam. Confidence is your stage light, costume is your armor, and silence is your nuclear deterrent. You don't need to be right—you just need to be unquestioned.

The smart ones fake it better than the real ones. This is how.

LESSON 1: Perception of Power, Authority, and Control

Tactic 1.1:
The Confidence Conspiracy: Power Is Theater

They told you power comes from hard work, degrees, loyalty— some noble fairy-tale bullshit HR cooked up to keep you punching a clock. Here's the truth: power's a costume. Whoever wears it best, wins. Nobody checks the stitching.

You can be broke, unqualified, and one bad week from eviction, but if you walk into that office like you own the damn air, people start holding their breath. They mistake nerve for destiny. That's the con. Power ain't about what you *are*; it's about what everybody else *thinks* you are.

It's like selling bottled water next to a running river. They still buy it, because you looked them dead in the eye and said, "This is the pure stuff." Confidence is the label; perception is the price tag.

Swagger Beats Substance

Look at your company's org chart. The top dog isn't the smartest one—he's the one with the loudest walk. The spreadsheet genius in the corner cubicle? Still waiting for someone to "notice his hard work." He'll die waiting.

The guy in the tailored jacket with a voice that cuts through noise like a car alarm—he's cashing bonuses off other people's silence. He don't need to know the answer; he just needs to sound too sure to question. People follow certainty the way flies follow light—they don't care if it burns them.

Confidence isn't proof. It's perfume—strong enough to cover the smell of fear. You marinate in it long enough, and even *you* start believing your own scent.

Inside the Scam

Here's how this con runs, step by step, every damn day in every boardroom from Wall Street to Walmart. The faker walks in slow. Doesn't rush, doesn't fidget. Claims the biggest chair before introductions even finish. Opens his mouth and drops a statement—short, final, absolute. *"We're doing this."* No question mark. Half the room nods out of reflex. The other half freezes, trying to remember who made him boss. Too late. He *is* the boss now, because nobody stopped him soon enough.

That's the confidence con in motion. Talk first, act certain, never backpedal. When they challenge you, double down. When they correct you, smirk like you planned the mistake. People mistake arrogance for authority because it's easier than admitting they've been hustled.

The Psychology of Followers

Humans crave a shepherd. They hate uncertainty more than they hate being wrong. So the one who *seems* sure becomes their anchor. Their brains turn off; their spines melt. You can see it happen—the slow nod, the eyes dropping, the note-taking starts. They're not thinking anymore; they're downloading orders.

That's why confidence spreads faster than flu. The more certain you sound, the more others repeat you, and repetition breeds belief. Before long, the lie you started as an act becomes company policy, brand identity, or political gospel.

They'll defend it for you. They'll fight to prove *you* were right, because admitting they were fooled would hurt worse. Congratulations— you've weaponized their pride.

The Illusion Becoming Real

Keep faking it long enough and the world starts bending to fit your story. That's when illusion becomes infrastructure. Your "gut decision" turns into a department memo. Your bluff becomes quarterly strategy. And everyone nods like they saw it coming all along.

You can almost taste it—the shift in the room when people stop challenging you and start seeking your approval. That's the moment swagger hardens into structure. From there, you don't lead by skill; you lead by inertia. The system protects its myth because it needs the myth to keep moving.

The Fallout

Every empire built on confidence has a body count. The quiet ones—the thinkers, the doubters—get flattened under the parade. They start copying your act or hating you for pulling it off. Doesn't matter. Either way, you win.

But here's the fine print most phonies never read: if you can't back the act *once in a while*, the mob will turn. One exposed bluff, and the same crowd that crowned you will light torches. You can fake the throne, but you still gotta defend it.

The Lesson

Stop waiting to be discovered. Stop treating humility like currency. Nobody's coming to promote your potential. You want the room? Take it. You want respect? Manufacture it. You want power? **Perform** it.

Because in this world, nobody's following the smartest person— they're following the one who looks too confident to question.

So put on the costume, sell the line, and keep your chin up while they buy the illusion.

Confidence is the only product that sells itself.

Tactic 1.2 :
The Costume of Authority: Costumes Make Kings

Authority isn't a fact. It's a costume. That shiny title, the corner office, the fancy pen in the velvet box — none of it proves jack.

But they'll bend a knee to it anyway because humans are lazy and symbols do the thinking for them. You put on the right shoes, the right watch, the right tone, and suddenly people stop checking receipts and start writing checks.

I've watched a janitor in a lab coat walk into a conference, shrug, say one sentence that sounded sciencey, and watch half the room flip into reverence like they just saw God. It wasn't magic. It was theater. The coat was the cue; the audience supplied the meaning. That's how authority spreads — not through competence, but through props and posture. The mask does the heavy lifting, and the crowd builds the mythology around it.

How Symbols Hijack Brains

Your brain is a pattern machine that hates work. Symbols are shortcuts. A badge, a title, a logo — those are mental flags that shout "trust me" without making anyone do the math. When a person shows the right symbols, the lazy part of the mind says, "safe," and that's it. No vetting, no due diligence, no follow-up questions.

That's the advantage of the costume: you don't have to be right if you look right. The room will fill in the rest. People will explain away mistakes because admitting they were fooled is worse for their ego than following a lie. They'll tell stories about how "he's always been like that" and "you just don't understand his vision." In other words, they do the PR for you. They patch the holes while you collect the checks.

Dressing Like Power — Not for Show, for Control

This ain't about shopping. It's strategic. The costume is anything that signals you're not one of the confused masses. It can be a physical thing — a blazer that fits, a leather folder, the right watch — or it can be ritual: walking in at the same minute, sending the same two-sentence email, never laughing at your own jokes. Consistency makes symbols sticky.

When you want to command, you layer: look the part, then act like the part's already true. Walk slow in the room. Let other people rush to fill the silence. Open your mail with an expression that says " I'm processing an empire" even if it's just a chain of complaints. Carry a quiet that reads as calculation, not cowardice. These small moves prime people to treat you differently — they'll whisper with less posture, they'll clear more space, and they'll hand you the floor without being asked.

The Rituals That Fake Respect Into Reality

Rituals bind people to narratives. Show up the same way every time. Call meetings that start at your time, not theirs. Send one-line directives that feel like orders. Make a signature move — a phrase, a gesture, a document — that becomes associated with action. The ritual is the costume's engine; it turns your act into expectation. Once expectation exists, obedience follows to avoid cognitive dissonance. People will conform because it's less painful than arguing with the rhythm you set.

And yes, some of it's petty. But petty works. People want to believe the show. Give them the show and they'll give you compliance.

When the Crowd Becomes Your Alibi

Here's the beautiful, dirty part: once you've got the costume and the ritual down, the crowd becomes your alibi. They'll defend decisions you didn't make, explain logic you never thought through, and manufacture rationale to protect the story. They'll invent competence to avoid being exposed for following a lie.

That's leverage. You don't have to justify yourself if other people are busy justifying you.

I saw a VP take credit for a project he whiteboarded half-heartedly and the team rewrote the history until his face looked heroic. Nobody wanted to admit they'd been led by a bluff. So they baked the bluff into the company myth. That myth becomes policy. That policy becomes your scaffolding.

How to Use the Costume Without Getting Burned

Don't be dumb — the costume's only as good as the hand that pulls the strings. If you dress like a king and can't deliver a single thing, the masks fall off and the same crowd that played along will light you up. The trick is to use the costume to buy you time to make something real. Do a small, undeniable thing to prove you mean it. A single good decision, a clean execution — that's enough to fuse the act to reality.

Also: never overshare the prop list. Don't explain why you do the rituals or why you wear the watch. Explanations break the spell. The less you reveal, the more they'll project.

The Anatomy of a Bulletproof Mask

A mask has three parts: symbol, rhythm, proof. The symbol gets attention — the title, the suit, the tone. Rhythm makes it predictable and unavoidable — the habitual entry, the signature sentence, the email cadence. Proof is that one action that convinces enough people to build a defense around you. You need all three to keep the crowd invested.

If one fails, the others can hold the lie slightly longer. If two fail, you're exposed. If none exist, you're honest—and in business, honesty without theater is a fast path to being ignored.

The Moral: No Ethics, Just Tactics

This is not a lecture on virtue. It's a field manual for people who want to run things. If you want applause for being "authentic," fine — that's a different market. But if you want influence, you use the costume. You step into the role someone else left vacant and make it stick. You do the ugly work of performance so others can feel safe in their follow-through.

Power loves preparation and performance more than truth. Learn the costume. Wear it when you need to. Use it to build something that outlasts the show — and when the show no longer serves you, take the mic down and walk away before they notice the wiring.

Tactic 1.3 :
Why the Powerful Never Explain Themselves

When you explain, you kneel. That's the whole truth. The minute you start defending yourself, you've already told the room you're not in charge. Power doesn't justify — it dictates. The king doesn't give a TED Talk about why he's on the throne. He just sits there while the peasants write myths about destiny.

Look around any boardroom, courtroom, or backroom deal — the one talking the most is the one losing control. The ones who shut up? They're the ones running the script. Silence forces the other side to fill the space with their own insecurity. The weak start rationalizing *your* decisions for you, trying to guess what you meant, why you said it, what you'll do next. That's how you own their heads without saying another word.

Mystery Beats Logic Every Damn Time

Power's favorite drug is ambiguity. People fear what they don't understand, and they respect what they can't predict. That's why

CEOs drop layoffs with a three-line memo, why politicians smirk instead of answering questions, and why gang leaders don't issue press releases. The mystery makes the myth. The less you say, the more they build your legend for you.

When you explain yourself, you give them handles — something to grab, twist, and use against you. When you don't, they chase shadows. They talk about you in hushed tones, trying to decode you like you're some oracle instead of a person who just decided not to give a damn.

The best part? People invent brilliance where none exists. "He must know something we don't." Nah — he just shut the fuck up while you kept talking.

Control the Air, Not the Words

You ever see a judge cut a lawyer off mid-sentence with a single raised eyebrow? That's the art. The words don't matter; the silence does. It's the pause, the space, the lack of reaction that breaks people down. They start overexplaining, apologizing, retreating into verbal quicksand. You don't need to attack when you can let them destroy themselves trying to fill your quiet.

The best manipulators weaponize that pause. They say something short, final, almost arrogant — then vanish into silence. "That's my decision." "It's handled." "I said what I said." No explanation. No justification. No energy wasted. Every extra sentence after that waters down your power like a whiskey drowned in ice.

Make Them Explain Themselves Instead

When someone demands answers, flip the damn table. Ask a question back. "Why do you need to know?" "What makes you think I care?" "Who told you I was taking suggestions?" Boom —

now *they're* the ones defending their curiosity, scrambling to justify their place in the conversation. It's psychological judo — let their own words throw them to the mat.

People crave structure, and when you withhold it, they start bending themselves into whatever shape they think you want. Keep your sentences short and your eyes steady. The more comfortable you are with silence, the more everyone else starts mistaking it for wisdom.

The Performance of Indifference

Indifference looks like godliness to the desperate. When you act like nothing shakes you, people assume you've seen behind the curtain. You become the one who "knows something." It doesn't matter if you're broke or bluffing — the vibe of calm detachment will make others orbit you like junkies around a dealer.

Power isn't loud. It's quiet. It's not about convincing — it's about *conditioning*. You don't win arguments; you make people stop believing they're worth your words. That's real dominance — not shouting louder, but being so still they start whispering.

Bottom Line: Say Less, Rule More

Explanations are confessions. The more you talk, the smaller you look. The powerful don't clarify, they *command*. When in doubt, say nothing. When pressed, say less. When cornered, ask questions until the other person gets tired of hearing themselves talk.

Your silence is the weapon. Your calm is the disguise. Your indifference is the noose. And by the time they realize the conversation was never mutual, it's too late — you already won it.

"Next: how you turn that swagger into addiction — how to make people move before they think!

> **Power doesn't come from credentials, titles, or IQ points. It comes from how well you fake the role until no one dares to question it. The truth is irrelevant. The costume matters more than the character. The tone matters more than the words. The silence matters more than the facts. Control is never given—it's performed, enforced, and defended like a territory. If you don't learn to wear the mask, someone else will put one on you. And trust me, it won't fit.**

Lesson 2: Psychological Influence & Manipulation

Tactic 2.1:
Emotion Is the Trigger

Logic's for Losers. Emotion Runs the Show. Let's stop pretending people are rational. Logic's the decorative mint on the pillow—looks nice, nobody touches it. Emotion runs every room, every vote, every sale, every fight. You don't win because you're right; you win because you made someone *feel* something first. Fear, lust, anger, envy—pick your poison. Once you hit the nerve, their brain checks out and you start driving the car.

You ever watch a salesman close a deal? He's not pitching numbers. He's whispering urgency—*this offer's ending today.* Watch a politician? He doesn't talk policy; he paints nightmares —*they're coming for your kids.* Preachers? They don't prove faith; they make you feel the fire. Every empire's been built on someone's emotional panic or hope. You can quote facts till you're blue in the face, but until you make the other person's stomach twist, you're just background noise.

Fear Beats Logic

Fear makes people stupid in record time. Tell someone the system's collapsing, and they'll buy your overpriced solution with trembling hands. Fear floods reason; it tells the brain, *don't think —move.* It's why the news screams headlines in all caps, why cults talk about apocalypse, why bosses "warn" about layoffs before asking for overtime. It's manipulation 101: get their heartbeat up, and you own their focus.

Anger Is the Easy Button

Rage is rocket fuel. When people get pissed, they don't verify— they charge. You don't have to argue if you can make them furious. Feed their resentment, whisper about how they've been "disrespected," and they'll do your fighting for you. It's how mob bosses build loyalty, how politicians rally voters, how managers deflect blame. Anger turns followers into soldiers.

Hope Is the Nicest Lie Ever Sold

Then there's hope—the prettiest scam in the world. Dangle "better days ahead," and you can make people swallow anything. It's how failing companies keep employees grinding, how lovers keep toxic relationships alive, how hustlers sell you dreams while stealing your wallet. Hope blinds more than fear ever could. It's optimism with a knife behind its back.

Emotion Is the Shortcut

Nobody wants to think. Thinking hurts. Emotion is the shortcut —the cheat code for control. You don't need proof; you need a pulse. Once they're reacting, not reasoning, you can steer them anywhere. The guy who understands this doesn't argue, doesn't beg, doesn't explain. He triggers, he watches, he directs.

Bottom line? Facts are for textbooks. Feelings are for power. You want control? Don't talk sense. Light a match in their gut and let them burn themselves into obedience.

Tactic 2.2:
Repetition & Charisma Are the Glue

Say it until they believe it. Smile while you do it. You hit them with emotion; now you keep them hooked. Emotion cracks the door. Repetition and charisma slam it open and nail it shut. One feeds the spark; the other makes the spark look like the sun. This is the slow burn — not an explosion, but the steady drumbeat that turns a lie into a hymn.

Repetition Is Religion

Humans hate thinking. Give them the same phrase enough times in enough arenas and their lazy brains will switch that phrase into a fact. That's the whole con. Advertisers, politicians, and snake-oil salesmen don't invent truth — they manufacture familiarity. Repetition builds a memory groove. Once something sits in the groove, intuition will defend it before reason has a voice.

You hear it in ad jingles that you can't shake. You see it in corporate slogans that show up in every email and every meeting until even your grandma believes in the mission. Say a line in a meeting, put it on a memo, echo it in a Slack, let your people say it on calls — soon enough they'll be parroting it in other rooms and you'll watch them stitch your narrative into the company wallpaper.

Repeat the same idea in slightly different clothes. Repetition isn't mindless parroting; it's strategic redundancy. You don't say the exact same sentence until people hate you — you phrase the same claim across contexts so their internal filters identify the pattern and stop questioning. Familiar = safe. Safe = true.

Charisma Is Contagion

Charisma isn't charm for the confused; it's a broadcast signal. It's the way someone's voice makes your gut stop doubting for a moment. It's posture like punctuation, delivery like proof. Charisma lets you sell the same recycled message in 20 different rooms and get the same obedience every single time.

It's not about being liked. It's about being memorable and making memory do the persuading work for you. A charismatic person can say something wildly incorrect and the room will rewrite their understanding around that lie. Why? Because charisma makes people *feel* like they're in on a secret. Feeling like you belong trumps being right. The charismatic operator understands how to position themselves as the axis of belonging.

Charisma is about timing, cadence, and small theatrics: the perfect pause before a line lands, the slight smile that makes a confession feel like a promise, the steady eye contact that removes doubt. These are performance tricks, not personality traits. Learn them, use them deliberately, don't confuse them with authenticity.

Repeat, Ritualize, Broadcast

This is a three-step loop: repeat the message, ritualize its delivery, broadcast it everywhere. Rituals make repetition sticky. A signature phrase, a consistent opening line, a recurring story — these are the anchors you drop into the collective mind. Rituals are rhythm: they create expectation. Expectation drowns out curiosity.

Broadcast is the messy part. Say it in the town hall, then put it on the memo, then tuck it into an email, then let influencers (your employees, your proxies) say it back. You want echo, not argument. The echo is your friend. Don't debate facts in public — repeat them until they're background noise.

The Small Moves That Work

- **Short phrases.** Keep the message dumb enough to spread. Complexity kills repeatability.

- **Ubiquity.** Drop the phrase across platforms and contexts. Email, meeting, social, hallway talk. Let it get everywhere.

- **Cadence.** Practice the delivery. Same words, different pace. Slow for gravitas, quick for urgency.

- **Signature story.** One short anecdote you tell over and over that illustrates the point. People remember stories when they forget facts.

- **Social proof seeding.** Get one person of influence to say it. Others will follow because copying saves effort.

Why People Defend the Echo

Once someone says the phrase, they're invested. They'll defend it to avoid cognitive dissonance. That's when repetition becomes a weapon beyond your control: others will fight for your line for their own sake. That's when your narrative gains immune response — criticism bounces off because it feels like people are protecting themselves, not you.

That's social contagion: ideas spread not because they're smart, but because parroting them reduces social friction. People align because it's easier than thinking.

When Charisma Masks Collapse

Here's the catch — repetition and charisma can sustain a hollow narrative, but only up to a point. If the structural proof collapses (missed deadlines, obvious incompetence), repetition will start to sound like a broken record. The charismatic leader can buy time, but they can't infinitely delay reality. So use repetition and charisma to create the runway — then land the plane. Deliver the small wins that prove the pattern.

If you don't, the same people who sang your hymn will march you out of the building with banners. Repetition and charm are amplifiers — powerful, but mortal.

Make It Loud, Make It Familiar

You don't win by educating people; you win by orchestrating what they hear until they think it was their idea. Repeat the phrase. Say it with feeling. Make it contagious. When people stop asking and start parroting, you stop persuading and start ruling. That's the dirty art of influence: not convincing minds, but hijacking them with rhythm and personality.

Tactic 2.3:
Dependency Is the Payoff

Addiction Is Control with a Smile. Here's the truth they don't print in leadership books: control ain't about domination or even respect. It's about dependency. The endgame isn't fear—it's addiction. The moment someone can't make a move without checking your reaction first, you've won. You don't need to shout, threaten, or demand. You just need to make yourself *necessary.* Once you become the oxygen in their room, they'll suffocate before they defy you.

Control Through Convenience

People aren't loyal to you. They're loyal to whatever makes their lives easier. That's the real choke chain. You want control? Become the shortcut. Be the person who "knows a guy," who "can handle it," who "makes things happen." Then sit back and watch them line up to depend on you.

That's how middle managers survive while smarter people get canned. The genius in the corner gets fired because no one notices him. The fixer—the one who's always in the loop, always got an answer—becomes indispensable. Nobody dares piss him off because losing him means chaos.

You don't need to own the company to run it. You just need to be the bridge everyone has to cross to get anything done. Control the gate, and you control the kingdom

Emotional Debt — The Invisible Chain

Favors are better than contracts. Do something for someone they didn't ask for, and they'll carry that weight like guilt they can't wash off. People *hate* being indebted. They'll pay you back in loyalty, obedience, and silence.

Play it smart: don't brag about what you did. Let them remember it. Let it rot in the back of their head until they can't look at you without feeling like they owe you. That's how cult leaders keep followers from leaving—emotional IOUs, layered with guilt, wrapped in gratitude.

You don't need to say "You owe me." The look alone will do it. The pause. The tone. The quiet reminder that you were there when no one else was. That's the leash. They'll pull it tighter themselves.

Scarcity: The Crack Cocaine of Control

Scarcity drives people insane. You never give them all of you. You drip-feed attention, approval, access—whatever currency you've got. The trick is to starve them just enough to make them chase.

Bosses do it with praise. Lovers do it with affection. Governments do it with hope. Give a little, take it back, make them earn the next hit. People don't crave abundance—they crave the high of getting *just enough.*

You want to be unforgettable? Be inconsistent. Be rare. Be the storm that visits only when it wants to. The more unpredictable you are, the more they orbit you. Scarcity turns you from a person into a goddamn event.

Make It Feel Like Their Idea

The most dangerous form of control is the kind that feels like freedom. You don't tell them what to do—you make them think they came up with it. Suggest, nudge, seed the thought, then step back. Let them build the prison and decorate it themselves.

That's how manipulators keep power for years. They let people believe they're "choosing" loyalty. It's an illusion, but it works because people are too proud to admit they're puppets.

You plant the thought: *"You're the only one I trust."* Boom—now they're loyal to prove you right.

You hint: *"You'd probably do it better your way."* Boom—now they're doing what you wanted while defending their independence.

Starve Them, Then Feed Them

The real pros know this move: disappear just long enough for the panic to set in. Pull away, go quiet, leave them hanging. They'll text, they'll fret, they'll spin stories in their head. Then you show back up calm, steady, and irreplaceable. Relief becomes gratitude, and gratitude becomes devotion. That's when they're hooked.

The more times you run that cycle—withdraw, return, reward—the stronger the dependency gets. You become the drug and the cure. They'll tolerate your bullshit, defend you against their better judgment, and call it "loyalty."

Bottom Line — Be the Habit, Not the Hero

Control doesn't come from intimidation. It comes from repetition, from wiring yourself into their emotional circuitry. You're not trying to be loved—you're trying to be *needed.*

Once they can't function without you, you can vanish for a week, fuck up royally, or make demands that sound insane—and they'll still crawl back because dependency kills pride before it kills habit.

That's the power nobody talks about. Not dominance. Not charisma. Addiction. Become the fix they can't quit, and they'll never see the strings even as they tighten around their neck.

Manipulation isn't about being evil. It's about being effective. The world doesn't respond to facts—it responds to emotions, repetition, and charisma. That's the game. The moment you realize that feelings outrank logic in every room, you stop arguing and start engineering. You don't ask for loyalty—you manufacture it. You don't wait for influence—you embed it. Anyone still trying to be "authentic" is playing the wrong sport. This is about control, not connection. And control always starts with belief.

Chapter Aftermath

You can quote Sun Tzu all you want, but the modern battlefield isn't blood and land—it's **attention and emotion**. The one who controls how people *feel* controls what they'll *do*, and the crowd never knows it's happening. The real generals don't carry guns anymore—they carry influence. They drop words instead of bombs and let repetition do the killing. Every commercial, every politician, every "motivational leader" is running the same psychological playbook—just prettier packaging.

This isn't morality; it's mechanics. Emotion is your entry point. Repetition cements belief. Charisma oils the gears. Dependency locks the cage. That's how psychological influence works—not as theory, but as daily commerce. You don't convince people— you *condition* them. You don't persuade—you *program*. Truth doesn't matter. Rhythm does. The pattern wins because it bypasses the brain and buries itself in reflex.

And if that makes you uncomfortable, good. That's the point. Discomfort is the moment you realize control isn't about force—it's about finesse. It's not who shouts loudest; it's who sets the beat everyone dances to. The game's been running your whole life. You just finally opened your eyes to who's holding the remote

CHAPTER TWO

Exploiting Psychological Weaknesses

*Welcome to Section 2—where we stop playing defense and start **weaponizing the fragile little cracks in human behavior** that most people don't even know they have. This isn't about charm, persuasion, or any of that feel-good, self-help bullshit. **This is psychological warfare where we hit them in the balls.** And in war, you don't just win—you make sure the other side never even knew they were in a fight.*

*While Chapter 1 was about understanding **power and influence**, Chapter 2 is where we get surgical. **People are walking, talking bundles of emotional weaknesses, just begging to be exploited.** They're insecure, desperate for validation, scared shitless of rejection, and addicted to the illusion of control. **Good. That's where we come in.***

Lesson 3: Finding Someone's Weak Spots

Tactic 3.1:
How to Spot Psychological Vulnerabilities in Minutes

People love to think they're complex, mysterious snowflakes. Spoiler alert: they're not. They're walking, talking bundles of insecurity wrapped in a thin layer of bullshit bravado. You don't need a PhD in psychology to figure them out—just a decent bullshit detector and the patience to watch them unravel.

Here's the thing: every motherfucker you meet has psychological weak spots, and they wear them like a neon sign if you know where to look. You don't need to dig deep. This isn't an archaeological excavation; it's more like tripping over a rock and realizing it's a landmine.

Want to spot vulnerabilities in minutes? Easy.

Step One: Listen for the asshole who won't shut up about how "confident" they are. That guy is softer than a wet napkin on the inside. Real confidence doesn't need a fucking megaphone.

Step Two: Watch for validation addicts. You know, the ones fishing for compliments like it's a sport. Give them a crumb of approval, then yank it back—they'll dance for it like a trained seal.

Step Three: Anyone who seems "too perfect" is hiding more red flags than a goddamn communist parade. Poke around, and you'll find the cracks faster than a cracked iPhone screen.

Where to Look:

1. **Listen for Insecurity Disguised as Confidence.**

   The loudest person in the room? Probably the most insecure. **Overcompensation is a dead giveaway.** The guy who brags about how "alpha" he is? Soft as wet tissue paper on the inside. People who are truly confident don't need to announce it.

2. **Watch for Validation Addicts.**

   If someone constantly seeks approval—**likes, compliments, reassurance—they're emotionally**

starving. Perfect. Now you know exactly how to feed them…and how to starve them when you want control.

3. **Spot the "Too Good to Be True" Personas.**

   The perfect partner, the flawless employee, the overly agreeable friend—**all masks.** No one's that polished unless they're hiding something underneath. Look for inconsistencies. **They'll slip up.**

4. **Identify Emotional Triggers in Conversations.**

   Mention certain topics and watch their body language. **Do they flinch? Get defensive? Ramble nervously?** That's not random. That's an emotional weak spot waving a red flag.

5. **Notice How They Handle Silence.**

   Most people are uncomfortable with silence. **They'll fill it with oversharing, nervous laughter, or backpedaling.** That's when they accidentally reveal more than they intended.

The Fastest Vulnerability Detector? Ego

Ego is the universal weak spot. Stroke it, and people will drop their guard. Challenge it, and they'll overreact. Either way, you win. **Finding vulnerabilities isn't about playing detective— it's about paying attention.** People show you exactly where to hit if you know what to look for. **The cracks are always there. Your job is to break them wide open.**

Tactic 3.2:
The Five Universal Human Weaknesses & How to Use Them

No matter how tough, smart, or self-aware someone thinks they are, **every human being comes with the same factory-installed flaws.** Call it emotional software. Some people just run the updates better than others. But underneath it all? **Everyone's got the same weak spots.** And if you know where to poke, you can control just about anyone.

Here are the **five universal human weaknesses**—the emotional pressure points that never fail. **Master these, and you'll never need to guess how to manipulate someone again.**

1. The Need for Validation

People are addicted to feeling "seen," "heard," and "valued." That's why social media exists—an endless loop of dopamine hits disguised as likes and comments. The average person's self-worth is hanging by a thread, and that thread is woven from the opinions of others.

How to Use It: Give them praise sparingly—like breadcrumbs. **Create dependency by making your approval rare and inconsistent.** The less you give, the more they chase it. This is the same trick casinos use with slot machines: unpredictable rewards keep people hooked. Compliment them when it benefits you, then withdraw it just enough to keep them guessing. **Confusion is the glue that holds manipulation together.**

2. Fear of Rejection

Rejection feels like death to the ego. It triggers primal panic because humans are hardwired to crave belonging. This isn't just emotional fluff—evolution made us this way. Back in caveman days, being rejected by the tribe meant you were probably going to die alone. That fear? **Still hardwired.**

How to Use It: Subtly threaten their sense of inclusion. **Withdraw attention. Act disinterested.** Even a slight pullback makes people scramble to "win you back," giving you the upper hand. In relationships, this is called "breadcrumbing." In business, it's called "leverage." In manipulation? **It's just Tuesday.**

3. The Desire for Control

Everyone thinks they're in control of their lives. **Spoiler: They're not.** But they crave the illusion of it because it makes them feel secure. People would rather believe they're steering the ship than admit they're just passengers on a sinking cruise.

How to Use It: Let them think they're steering the ship while you're controlling the waters. Offer choices that all lead where *you* want them to go. Want them to pick Option A? Present it alongside a garbage Option B and an absurd Option C. Suddenly, Option A feels like their "smart decision," even though it's exactly what you wanted from the start. **This is how "freedom" works in marketing, politics, and relationships.**

4. Fear of Missing Out (FOMO)

Nothing triggers anxiety faster than the idea that someone else has something they don't. **People aren't afraid of losing out on something—they're afraid someone else is winning without them.** That's why scarcity sells. It's not about value; it's about the panic that someone else is getting what you're not.

How to Use It: Create artificial scarcity. Make your time, attention, or whatever you're offering seem exclusive. Limited spots. One-time offers. *"I'm not sure if I'll have time for this later."* People don't want things because they're valuable—they want them because they think they can't have them. **Scarcity flips their logical brain off like a light switch.**

5. The Need to Feel "Special"

People want to believe they're unique, exceptional, one-of-a-kind snowflakes. **Newsflash: They're not.** But that belief is the ultimate ego lever. They'll do mental gymnastics to protect it because their entire identity is built on the lie that they're somehow different from everyone else.

How to Use It: Flatter strategically. Not the obvious kind—skip the *"You're amazing!"* bullshit. Instead, make it feel personal. *"I don't usually share this, but you're sharp enough to get it."* That little whisper of exclusivity hooks them deeper than any compliment. **Once they feel special, they'll do damn near anything to keep feeling that way.**

The Dark Side Bonus: Stack the Weaknesses

Here's where it gets fun: **these weaknesses aren't isolated—they're stackable.**

- ◉ **Need for validation + fear of rejection?** You've got someone who'll chase your approval like it's oxygen.

- ◉ **Desire for control + FOMO?** Easy to push them into decisions they think they made on their own.

- ◉ **Fear of rejection + need to feel special?** You can make them beg to be part of your world.

The more weaknesses you layer, the stronger the leash. It's not manipulation if they hand you the rope willingly.

The Bottom Line: Everyone's got these weaknesses. No exceptions. Your job isn't to fix them—it's to **exploit them.** And once you do, you'll realize something terrifying: **most people aren't hard to control—they're practically begging for it.**

Tactic 3.3:
The Dependency Cycle: How to Make & Keep People Hooked

You don't control people by force. That's sloppy, inefficient, and burns out fast. Real control—the kind that lasts—is built through **dependency.** Make them rely on you, make them need you, and they won't just accept your influence—**they'll defend it, justify it, and cling to it like a life raft.**

The trick? **You don't just create dependency—you create a cycle.** A loop where they crave your attention, validation, and approval, even when it's you pulling the strings that keep them unstable. **Push, pull, reward, punish—repeat until they think life without you is unthinkable.**

How to Build an Unbreakable Dependency Cycle:

1. Solve Problems They Didn't Know They Had

Before someone can depend on you, **they need a reason to.**

- Point out a "flaw" they hadn't noticed: *"You're really talented, but you could be so much more with the right guidance."*

- Create a gap: *"Most people in your field already know this... You haven't learned it yet?"*

- Offer yourself as the solution: *"Don't worry, I can help you with that."*

Step One: *You invent the problem.*
Step Two: *You sell the cure.*

2. Give Just Enough to Keep Them Wanting More

A starving person will chase crumbs if you throw them just right.

- Never give full validation—make them work for it. *"You're getting there."*

- Withdraw approval unpredictably. Praise them one day, then act indifferent the next.

- Let them feel your absence. **Pull back just enough that they start craving your attention.**

This taps into the same psychology as gambling: **random rewards keep people addicted.**

3. Control Access to Something They Value

Make yourself the gatekeeper to what they want.

- **In business?** Be the one with the connections, the industry secrets, the missing piece.

- **In relationships?** Make them believe you "understand" them in a way no one else does.

- **In social circles?** Position yourself as the hub of influence—cutting you off means cutting off their access.

The moment they feel like **you're the bridge to what they need,** they'll never want to burn it.

4. Play the Emotional Yo-Yo—Highs and Lows Keep Them Hooked

Emotional stability is the enemy of control. Keep them guessing.

- One day, be warm, supportive, and affirming.
- The next? Cold, distant, disinterested.
- When they ask what's wrong, act like nothing's changed.

This forces them to chase the version of you they thought they had. They'll work harder, try to "fix" things, and unknowingly dig themselves deeper into dependence.

5. Turn Their Gratitude Into Emotional Debt

Do them a favor—but make sure they never forget it.

- ◉ *"I don't usually do this for people, but I see potential in you."*

- ◉ *"I stayed up late helping you. Just remember who had your back."*

- ◉ *"I fought for you when no one else would."*

Now, **they owe you.** And the longer they stay, the harder it gets to leave, because leaving means admitting they were used. **Most people would rather stay in the trap than admit they walked into it willingly.**

The Bottom Line: Dependency isn't about love, trust, or even fear—it's about making them believe they can't function without you. Keep them reaching, keep them second-guessing, and keep yourself positioned as the one thing in their life that makes sense. **They won't just stay—they'll fight to prove they belong.** And that's when you own them.

Tactic 3.4:
Using Their Own Self-Doubt Against Them

You don't need to break people. Most of them are already broken—they just do a damn good job pretending they're not. **Self-doubt is the crack in the armor, and all you have to do is pry it open.** The best part? You don't even have to plant the doubt. **It's already there.** Your job is to **amplify it until they can't hear anything else.**

Here's the ugly truth: Everyone has that little voice in their head whispering, *"You're not good enough,"* or *"What if they find* *out you're a fraud?"* You don't need to shout over it. **You just need to agree with it.** Subtly. Strategically. Consistently. Before long, **their biggest enemy isn't you—it's their own reflection.**

How to Turn Self-Doubt Into Your Personal Puppet Strings:

1. Ask Loaded Questions That Trigger Insecurity

Forget arguing or criticizing. **A well-timed question is more destructive than any insult.**

- *"Are you sure that's the best approach?"*
- *"Do you really think you're qualified for that?"*
- *"Has that ever worked out for you before?"*

You're not attacking them—you're letting **them attack themselves.** Doubt thrives when it feels self-generated.

2. Use Backhanded Compliments

Praise with a blade hidden inside. Make it sound supportive while subtly pointing out their flaws.

- *"Wow, you're actually really articulate for someone without formal training."*
- *"You did great—way better than I expected."*

  It's not enough to insult them outright. **You want them questioning if it was even an insult at all.** That's the sweet spot where self-doubt festers.

3. Mirror Their Insecurities Back at Them

People drop hints about their insecurities all the time—**you just have to listen.**

- If they constantly talk about being "misunderstood," casually reinforce it: *"Yeah, I get that. Sometimes your ideas do come off a little...unclear."*

- If they obsess over being "overlooked," plant the seed: *"I was surprised you got picked for that. Thought they'd go with someone more experienced."*

You're not introducing new insecurities—you're feeding the ones they already have.

4. Subtle Comparisons

Nothing eats at people faster than feeling inferior.

- *"John handled that project effortlessly. You're doing it differently, though, right?"*

- *"She's a natural at that. But you've got your own style."*

Notice the trick? **You're not insulting them—you're just casually highlighting that someone else might be better.** They'll do the rest of the work, comparing themselves into oblivion.

5. Use Silence as a Doubt Amplifier

Sometimes, saying nothing is more powerful than saying anything.

- When they expect praise, give them nothing. Let them sit in the silence, wondering if they messed up.

- When they seek reassurance, just nod. No words. Let their brain spiral into overthinking mode.

Silence isn't empty—it's a psychological pressure cooker.

The Long Game: Let Them Destroy Themselves

You're not the villain in their story. You're just the narrator, gently pointing out flaws they already noticed but hoped no one else would see.

- ◉ **Plant the seed of doubt.**

- ◉ **Water it with subtle reminders.**

- ◉ **Watch it grow into a full-blown identity crisis.**

They'll start second-guessing everything—**their choices, their skills, their worth.** And when they hit rock bottom, guess who they'll turn to for validation, reassurance, and guidance? **You.** Because nothing builds control like convincing someone they can't trust themselves.

Self-doubt isn't just a weakness—it's a weapon. The best part? You don't even have to pull the trigger. They'll do it for you.

Power doesn't come from credentials, titles, or IQ points. It comes from how well you fake the role until no one dares to question it. The truth is irrelevant. The costume matters more than the character. The tone matters more than the words. The silence matters more than the facts. Control is never given—it's performed, enforced, and defended like a territory. If you don't learn to wear the mask, someone else will put one on you. And trust me, it won't fit.

Lesson 4: Emotional Triggers and Manipulation

Tactic 4.1:
The Fear and Scarcity Effect: How to Trigger Panic and
Control Decisions

Forget inspiration. Fear is the only thing that truly **controls** people. You don't get them to move, comply, or beg for your approval by giving motivational speeches. You do it by grabbing them by the fucking throat with fear and squeezing until they make the exact decision you want. Add scarcity to the mix, and you've got a psychological chokehold that most people are too weak to break.

Here's the truth most assholes don't want to admit: **fear runs the world.** It overrides logic, burns confidence to the ground, and leaves people in a frenzy, desperate for a way out. And guess who controls the only escape route? You.

The best part? **The fear doesn't even have to be real.** People don't respond to actual danger—they respond to **the idea of it.** You can make them panic over a goddamn shadow if you cast it the right way.

How to Weaponize Fear and Scarcity Like a Pro:

1. Trigger Fear Through Uncertainty

Certainty breeds confidence. Uncertainty breeds fear.

- Be vague: *"I'm not sure how this will work out for you."*

- Plant doubt: *"People are starting to question your reliability."*

- Create ambiguity: *"We'll have to see what happens."*

Uncertainty forces the mind into overdrive, filling in the blanks with worst-case scenarios. The less you say, the scarier it gets—because the fear lives in their head, not your words.

2. Threaten Loss Without Direct Threats

You don't need to say, "I'll take this away." That's too obvious.

- ◉ *"I thought you were the right person for this, but I'm not sure anymore."*

- ◉ *"There are others who'd kill for this opportunity."*

Now they're scrambling—not because you took something from them, but because you made them feel like they're about to lose it. Fear of potential loss hits harder than the loss itself.

3. Use Scarcity to Create Urgency

People don't want what's abundant. They want what's disappearing.

- *"This offer won't be available for long."*
- *"I only have limited spots for this."*
- *"I can't promise I'll have time for this later."*

Even if it's bullshit, it works. Scarcity taps into primal instincts—if something is rare, it must be valuable. And if it's about to be gone, people will act before they think.

4. Play with Social Scarcity–Fear of Being Left Out

It's not just about missing out on things–it's about missing out while someone else gets it.

- ◉ *"Everyone else has already signed up. I assumed you'd be the first."*

- ◉ *"I thought you'd be ahead of the curve, but others jumped on this faster."*

Now it's not just FOMO—it's *fear of being the loser*. And nothing drives people harder than the ego hit of thinking someone else beat them to the punch.

5. Use Inconsistent Reassurance to Keep Them Hooked

Too much fear causes paralysis. The trick is to sprinkle in just enough hope to keep them chasing.

- Give mixed signals: *"I believe in you, but..."*

- Offer crumbs of validation: *"You handled that well—let's see if you can keep it up."*

This keeps them in a constant loop of anxiety and relief, like a psychological slot machine. They never know when they'll get the payoff, so they keep playing. And the house always wins.

The Bottom Line

Fear makes people move. Scarcity makes them move faster. You don't need to be loud, aggressive, or even truthful—just create the illusion that something is at risk. Because people aren't afraid of what they've lost. They're afraid of what they *might* lose—and that's where you keep them: one step away from panic, running straight into your control.

Tactic 4.2:
Emotional Triggers: How Jealousy, Guilt, and Shame Keep People in Check

You don't need chains to control people—just the right emotional trigger. Forget brute force. The most effective way to keep someone in line is to make them their own warden. **Jealousy, guilt, and shame are the psychological holy trinity of manipulation.** You don't have to do the heavy lifting because their own emotions will choke them out while you sit back and watch.

Here's the beauty of it: **these emotions feel personal.** People don't think they're being manipulated because it feels like *their* feelings. **That's the trick.** You're not shoving them into a cage—you're handing them the key and convincing them to lock the door themselves.

1. Weaponizing Jealousy: Make Them Desperate to Compete

Jealousy is rooted in comparison, and people can't help but measure themselves against others.

- *"It's crazy how well John handled that project. I thought you'd be ahead of him by now."*

- *"I was talking to someone who's way less experienced than you, and even they figured it out."*

This isn't a compliment sandwich—it's a comparison knife. You're not just highlighting someone else's success; you're framing it as their failure. The result? They'll work harder, not to improve—but to outshine whoever you just mentioned. **You didn't inspire them. You infected them with insecurity.**

2. Guilt: The Invisible Leash

Guilt makes people apologize for things they didn't even do wrong. The best part? You don't have to accuse them of anything—just imply they let you down.

- *"I really expected more from you."*

- *"After everything I've done for you, I thought you'd handle this differently."*

Now they're not just trying to make things right—they're trying to make *you* feel better. **They become obsessed with earning back your approval, even if they never actually lost it.**

3. Shame: The Nuclear Option

Guilt is about feeling bad for what you did. Shame is about feeling bad for who you are. And that's where the real power lies.

- *"I thought you were smarter than this."*

- *"I guess I gave you too much credit."*

Shame attacks their identity, not their actions. It doesn't make them feel like they made a mistake—it makes them feel like *they are* the mistake. And people will jump through emotional hoops to escape that feeling, often doing exactly what you want without realizing why.

4. The Emotional Whiplash Effect: Mix, Match, and Confuse

The real magic happens when you **rotate these emotions like a psychological washing machine.**

- Praise them briefly, then hit them with comparison-induced jealousy.

- Offer support, then slip in guilt: *"I just thought you'd be more reliable."*

- Build them up, then drop subtle shame: *"Wow, I really misjudged your potential."*

This emotional chaos keeps them disoriented, always chasing your validation. They never know if they're winning or losing, which means **you're always the one keeping score.**

The Bottom Line:

You don't control people by forcing them into submission. You control them by turning their emotions against them. Jealousy makes them compete, guilt makes them compliant, and shame makes them question their very existence.

And the best part? They'll never blame you for it. They'll blame themselves.

Tactic 4.3:
Why People Will Defend Their Own Manipulation

People are stupidly loyal to the very things that screw them over. It's one of the easiest psychological glitches to exploit. **You don't have to hide your manipulation—you just have to convince them it's their idea.** Hell, even when they catch on, most people will defend you, justify your behavior, and fight to protect the illusion you've built. **Why? Because admitting they've been manipulated feels worse than the manipulation itself.**

Here's the harsh reality: Nobody wants to admit they've been played. **It bruises the ego, shatters their sense of control, and makes them feel like an idiot.** So instead of facing that uncomfortable truth, they do what humans do best—**they double down on the lie.** They'll rationalize your behavior, twist reality to fit their narrative, and even attack anyone who points out the obvious. **You don't have to be a master manipulator— you just have to let their pride do the heavy lifting.**

How to Make People Defend Your Manipulation:

1. Give Them Just Enough "Wins" to Feel In Control

People love feeling like they're in charge, even when they're not.

- ◉ *"I value your opinion on this."*

- ◉ *"You're the only one I trust with this decision."*

Translation: *"I'm letting you pick from the options I've already decided on."* But they'll feel empowered, completely oblivious to the fact that **you've been steering the ship the entire time.**

2. Wrap Manipulation in Flattery

Nothing disarms suspicion like a well-placed compliment.

- *"You're too smart to fall for the kind of games other people play."*

- *"I respect how independent you are—I'd never try to control you."*

Congratulations. You've just manipulated them into believing they're unmanipulatable. **It's like putting a "Do Not Enter" sign on an open door—and watching them walk right through it.**

3. Use Emotional Investment Against Them

The more time, energy, or emotion someone invests, **the harder they'll fight to defend it.**

- *"After everything we've been through, you know I'd never lie to you."*

- *"Think about how far we've come—I wouldn't risk that."*

Now they're not just defending you—they're defending their own decisions. **It's not about protecting you. It's about protecting themselves from feeling stupid.**

4. Shift the Blame Subtly

Never take the hit directly. Deflect, redirect, and let them do the mental gymnastics.

- *"I think you're overthinking it."*

- *"Maybe you're just being too sensitive."*

Suddenly, it's not your fault—they're the problem for even questioning it. **Gaslighting? Sure. But with a side of charm to keep it palatable.**

5. Create an "Us vs. Them" Dynamic

The best way to keep someone loyal is to give them an enemy that isn't you.

- *"They're just jealous of what we have."*

- *"People don't understand because they don't know the full story."*

Now, anyone who points out your manipulation looks like the bad guy. **You don't even have to defend yourself—your victim will do it for you.**

You don't have to be perfect at manipulating people. You just have to understand one thing—people would rather protect a lie than admit they've been living one.
All you have to do is sit back and let their ego do the dirty work. **And trust me, it will.**

> *Manipulation isn't about being evil. It's about being effective. The world doesn't respond to facts—it responds to emotions, repetition, and charisma. That's the game. The moment you realize that feelings outrank logic in every room, you stop arguing and start engineering. You don't ask for loyalty—you manufacture it. You don't wait for influence— you embed it. Anyone still trying to be "authentic" is playing the wrong sport. This is about control, not connection. And control always starts with belief.*

Lesson 5: Controlling the Emotional Battlefield

Tactic 5.1:

Conversational Manipulation: How to Set Traps & Keep People Chasing You

Conversations aren't about connection. That's a fairytale people tell themselves to feel special. The truth? **Conversations are battles.** Some people walk in with honesty and "open hearts." **You're walking in with a psychological sledgehammer.** The goal isn't to bond—it's to dominate, control, and leave the other person wondering if they're the crazy one.

The trick? Make it look casual. No dramatic speeches. No villain monologues. **Just small, seemingly harmless comments that act like emotional landmines—one wrong step, and boom.** You've got them doubting themselves, seeking your approval, or bending over backward to "fix" something they didn't even break.

How to Set Conversational Traps Like a Pro:

1. The Loaded Question Trap

Ask questions that are basically psychological grenades with the pin already pulled.

- *"Why do you think people don't take you seriously?"*

- *"When did you realize you're not as confident as you pretend to be?"*

No matter how they answer, they're screwed. Deny it? They sound defensive. Admit it? They've just exposed their own insecurities. **It's like handing someone a shovel and watching them dig their own hole.**

2. The Compliment-Backhand Combo

Start with praise, then slap them with a hidden insult.

- *"You're surprisingly articulate for someone with no real experience."*
- *"I admire your boldness—it's impressive, even when it's completely misplaced."*

They'll spend the rest of the conversation trying to decode whether it was a compliment or an insult. **Spoiler: It was both. And that confusion keeps them off-balance—right where you want them.**

3. The False Choice Trap

Give them options, but both suck.

- *"Would you say your biggest flaw is being indecisive or overly sensitive?"*
- *"Are you more frustrated by your lack of focus or your inability to follow through?"*

They'll pick one because they think they're making a choice. **But here's the joke—you've already framed them as flawed.** No matter what they say, **you win.**

4. The Emotional Push-Pull Game

Give them attention, then rip it away like a psychological yo-yo.

- Be engaged, attentive, and charming.
- Then suddenly go cold, distant, and disinterested.

This triggers **emotional whiplash**. They'll start chasing your approval, wondering what they did wrong, desperate to get back in your good graces. **And they'll never realize it was all part of the plan.**

5. The Silence Pressure Cooker

Say something that stings, then shut up.

- ⦿ *"That's an interesting perspective…"* **[Pause. Stare. Wait.]**

- ⦿ *"I thought you'd handle that better."* **[Silence. Watch them squirm.]**

Most people can't handle silence. They'll rush to fill the gap with over-explanations, justifications, or nervous babbling— **accidentally revealing more than they ever intended.** You just sit there and let the silence do the work. **It's free real estate.**

6. The Emotional Bait-and-Switch

Drop a casual emotional trigger, then act like it's no big deal.

- ⦿ *"It's funny how people overcompensate when they're insecure."*

- ⦿ *"I've noticed people who talk the most usually feel the least confident."*

If it hits a nerve, you'll see it—a micro-expression, a slight shift, a flash of defensiveness. **Boom. Target acquired.** Now you know exactly where to dig.

The Bottom Line:

Conversations aren't for exchanging ideas—they're for planting psychological landmines. Every word is bait, every question a trap, and every silence a loaded gun.

The goal isn't to win the conversation. It's to make sure they never realize they lost.

Tactic 5.2:
Using Small Wins to Build Massive Control Over Time

Control isn't about grand gestures or dramatic power moves. That's amateur shit. The real masters? They build control the same way you gain weight—**one small, unnoticed bite at a time.** It's not about the big wins; it's the tiny victories that pile up until one day, without realizing it, **someone's completely under your thumb, wondering how the hell they got there.**

You don't walk in and take over someone's mind like a Bond villain. **You chip away at their independence, inch by inch, until they're basically running your emotional errands without a clue.** Think of it like psychological Jenga—**you remove just enough pieces to destabilize them, but not enough for them to notice until the whole thing collapses.**

How to Use Small Wins to Build Massive Control:

1. Get Them to Agree to Little Things First

People hate being inconsistent. If you can get them to say "yes" to something small, they're more likely to keep saying "yes" just to avoid cognitive dissonance.

- ◉ *"Hey, can you help me with this quick thing?"*
- ◉ *"Mind reviewing this for me?"*

It starts as a favor. **Before they know it, they're basically your unpaid intern.** Congratulations.

2. Create Micro-Dependencies

Don't go for total control right away. **Create tiny points of dependency.**

- You become the person they always vent to.
- The one who "understands" them better than anyone else.
- The go-to for advice they could've figured out themselves.

They think you're supportive. What they don't realize is you're slowly rewiring their emotional GPS to point straight to you.

3. Use Positive Reinforcement–But Inconsistently

Consistency is for dog trainers. You want to hook someone? **Be unpredictable.** Reward them occasionally, then pull back.

- Compliment them once, then ignore them the next time.
- Show interest, then act distant.

This taps into the same psychological trap as slot machines— **the randomness keeps them addicted, always chasing the next "win."**

4. Frame Your Influence as Their Idea

People are easier to control when they think it's their decision.

- Instead of saying, *"Do this,"* say, *"What do you think about doing this?"*
- Make suggestions sound like discoveries: *"I noticed something that might help you..."*

Now they feel empowered, **completely unaware you're the one writing the script.**

5. Stack the Wins, Then Flip the Leverage

Every small "yes," every tiny favor, every little moment of reliance adds up. **By the time they realize how much they depend on you, it's too late.**

- They'll justify your influence.

- They'll defend your control.

- **Hell, they'll probably thank you for it.**

Big moves get attention. Small wins build empires. You don't conquer someone's mind overnight. **You just keep winning little battles until one day, you look around—and you own the whole damn war.**

And the best part? **They'll think it was their idea all along.**

Tactic 5.3:
The Confusion Strategy—How to Spot, Exploit, and Keep People Off-Balance

You want to control someone? Don't give them clarity—give them confusion. Clarity leads to confidence, and confident people are hard to manipulate. **But confused people? They're emotional Play-Doh—soft, malleable, and easy to shape into whatever you need.**

Here's the ugly truth: People hate feeling confused so much that they'll accept any explanation, no matter how ridiculous, just to make it stop. **That's your in.** When their brain is busy trying to make sense of the chaos, **they're not questioning you.** They'll follow the loudest voice, the simplest answer, the first person who offers certainty—**even if that certainty is total bullshit.**

How to Weaponize Confusion Like a Pro:

1. Flood Them with Contradictory Information

Nothing scrambles the brain faster than mixed signals.

- Compliment them one day: *"You're amazing at this."*

- Criticize them the next: *"Honestly, I expected more from you."*

It keeps them off-balance, wondering where they stand. **And when people are unsure, they cling to the source of their confusion—you.** Congratulations, you're now their emotional compass. Spoiler: **You're pointing them in circles.**

2. Answer Questions with More Questions

When someone seeks clarity, **don't give it to them.** Instead, respond with vague, open-ended questions:

- *"Why do you think that's important?"*

- *"What makes you feel that way?"*
  This forces them to do the mental heavy lifting while you sit back and watch them unravel. **Confusion isn't a lack of answers—it's an overload of possibilities.**

3. Change the Rules Mid-Game

Keep shifting expectations so they never feel secure.

- In relationships? Be affectionate, then distant.

- In business? Change deadlines, priorities, or standards without warning.

They'll waste so much energy trying to adapt that they'll stop questioning why the rules keep changing. **Hint: It's because you keep changing them.**

4. Use "Word Salad" to Overwhelm Them

Over-explain everything until their brain short-circuits.

- Ramble about irrelevant details.

- Use jargon, big words, or convoluted logic.

The goal isn't to make sense—it's to make them feel stupid for not "getting it." Eventually, **they'll just nod along, agreeing to avoid the mental exhaustion.**

5. Flip the Script When They Get Close to the Truth

If they start catching on? **Accuse *them* of being the problem.**

- *"You're overthinking this."*

- *"I don't know why you're making things complicated."*
  Suddenly, **they're defending themselves instead of questioning you.** That's not just misdirection—that's psychological sleight of hand.

The Bottom Line:

Control isn't about having the right answers—it's about making sure no one else does.

Keep people confused, keep them guessing, and they'll never realize **you've been pulling the strings the whole time. Because nothing's easier to control than someone who's too dizzy to stand on their own.**

Tactic 5.4:

The Dependency Cycle—How Emotional Chaos & Control Keep People Hooked

You don't control people with kindness. That's for therapists, life coaches, and other overpriced motivational frauds. You control people the same way drug dealers control junkies—**by getting them hooked, keeping them unstable, and making sure you're the only thing that feels like relief.** Comfort? Security? Stability? **That shit's for amateurs.** You want real power? **You turn someone's emotions into a carnival ride—no seatbelt, no safety bar, just pure chaos.**

Here's the brutal truth: People aren't addicted to happiness. **They're addicted to hope.** Hope that things will get better, hope that *you'll* get better, hope that the emotional roller coaster isn't actually headed off a cliff. **Newsflash: It is—and you're the one driving.** The trick isn't making them feel good. **It's making them feel just good enough to keep coming back, like rats in an emotional maze, chasing a piece of cheese that doesn't even exist.**

How to Build the Dependency Cycle:

1. Love-Bomb, Then Withdraw

Start with overwhelming attention—make them feel like the center of the universe. Compliments, constant contact, emotional fireworks. They'll get addicted fast.

- *"I've never met anyone like you."*
- *"I can't stop thinking about you."*

And just when they're hooked? **Disappear.** Go cold. Ignore them.

Now they're confused, anxious, desperate to "fix" whatever they think went wrong. **Spoiler: Nothing went wrong. That's the point.**

2. Create Emotional Highs and Lows

Consistency breeds security. Insecurity breeds dependency.

- One day, you're warm and supportive.

- The next? Distant and disinterested.

This emotional whiplash keeps them off-balance, always chasing the version of you they *thought* they had. **It's like gambling—they keep pulling the lever, hoping for the jackpot that never comes.**

3. Give Them "Hope Breadcrumbs"

Never cut them off completely. That's not control—that's abandonment.

- Send a random, sweet message after days of silence: *"Hey, just thinking about you."*

- Offer vague reassurances: *"Things have just been crazy. We'll talk soon."*

Hope is the drug. You don't give them the full dose—just enough to keep them addicted.

4. Make Yourself the Solution to the Problem You Created

Here's the real genius: **create the emotional chaos, then offer yourself as the cure.**

- Cause insecurity, then comfort them.

◉ Trigger jealousy, then reassure them.

They'll associate relief with you, not realizing **you're the one causing the pain in the first place.** It's like setting a fire and selling the water.

5. Reinforce the Cycle with Guilt and Gratitude

When they finally question things? **Flip it. Make them feel guilty.**

◉ *"I've done so much for you. Why are you being distant?"*

◉ *"I thought you appreciated me more than this."*

Now they're apologizing for reacting to the chaos *you* created. **That's not just control—that's ownership.**

Dependency isn't built on love. It's built on uncertainty, anxiety, and hope. Keep them guessing, keep them chasing, and before long, **you're not just part of their life—you're the only part that feels real. And the best part? They'll thank you for it.**

> *Jealousy is a loaded gun. All you have to do is hand it to them and let their imagination pull the trigger. You don't need to lie—you just need to let them fill in the blanks. The fear of losing you is more powerful than anything you could say out loud. It's not about cheating. It's about suggestion. It's about walking the line between availability and mystery until their paranoia becomes your puppet. The more insecure they feel, the more control you hold. And if they start accusing you? Congratulations. That means it's working.*

Chapter Aftermath

You've seen the playbook now — how people hand over their sanity for scraps of validation, how fear makes them sprint into the leash and call it leadership, how confusion and dependency wrap around them like silk rope. Don't kid yourself — this isn't theory. This is the battlefield you walk through every damn day wearing a smile.

Power isn't about muscles or money — it's about getting inside someone's head and rearranging the furniture until they forget where the doors are. That's the game. You pull the strings, they thank you for it. You disappear, they panic. You return, they worship. That's not influence — that's ownership.

And here's the ugly cherry on top: once you learn to see these weaknesses, you can't unsee them. Every conversation, every handshake, every "trust me" turns into a diagnostic scan. You start spotting fractures in real time — and the more you do, the harder it is to believe in anything genuine again. That's the price of knowing.

So walk carefully. Use it or don't — but understand this: once you've weaponized human emotion, there's no going back. You're not playing defense anymore. You're behind the curtain now, where the real strings get pulled.

Welcome to the other side of control.

CHAPTER THREE

<u>The Puppet Masters Playbook</u>

Welcome to the dark arts of psychological warfare—where truth is optional, reality is negotiable, and facts are just inconvenient speed bumps. This chapter isn't about persuasion or influence. **That's for amateurs.** This is about **control.** Not the kind where people know they're being manipulated—that's sloppy. **Real control is invisible.** It's the kind where people defend you, fight for you, and swear on their lives that every decision they made was their own... even though you orchestrated every move.

In **The Puppet Master's Playbook,** you'll learn how to **gaslight, deceive, reframe reality, and make your version of the story the only one that matters.** This isn't about lying with a straight face—it's about making them question if they even knew the truth to begin with. **You don't just tell lies. You build them into the foundation of someone's thinking.**

Lesson Six: Gaslighting 101–Rewriting Reality

Tactic 6.1:
The Psychology Behind Gaslighting — Why It Works

Gaslighting isn't just manipulation — it's psychological arson. You're not debating. You're not convincing. **You're setting fire to someone's reality and handing them the matches, making them believe they lit it themselves.** That's the beauty of gaslighting: it doesn't work because you're a genius liar; it works because people are desperate to believe their own minds are reliable. **Spoiler alert: They're not.**

Here's why gaslighting works so well: The human brain is lazy. It's a pattern-recognition machine that cuts corners wherever it can. **Instead of thinking critically, it looks for shortcuts — emotional cues, social validation, consistency.** Gaslighting exploits all of that. You don't need facts. You don't even need to be convincing. **You just need to create enough doubt that their brain does the dirty work for you.**

The Core Psychological Principles Behind Gaslighting:

1. People Crave Certainty–Even If It's a Lie

The human mind hates ambiguity like a cat hates water. When faced with uncertainty, people will accept almost any explanation just to make the discomfort stop.

- *"You're overreacting."*
- *"That's not what happened."*
- *"You always twist things."*

It doesn't have to be true. **It just has to be said with confidence.** Their brain will fill in the blanks, convincing them that *maybe* they really are overreacting.

2. Repetition Beats Reality

Say something enough times, and it becomes "true." This isn't magic—it's neuroscience. The more the brain hears something, the more familiar it feels, and **familiarity feels like truth.**

- *"You've always been bad with details."*

- *"You're just too sensitive."*

Eventually, **they'll start repeating it back to themselves.** That's when you know you've won—not when they believe *you*, but when they doubt *themselves* without your help.

3. The Emotional Hook: Guilt, Shame, and Insecurity

Gaslighting doesn't just target thoughts—it targets feelings. **Guilt and shame are psychological superglue.**

- Make them feel guilty: *"I can't believe you'd think that about me after everything I've done for you."*

- Make them feel ashamed: *"Wow, I didn't realize you were that paranoid."*

People will do anything to escape guilt and shame, including rewriting their own memories to match the narrative you've fed them.

4. Isolation Amplifies Doubt

The fewer people they can check reality with, the more powerful your influence becomes.

- *"Don't tell anyone about this—they'll just make things worse."*

- *"Your friends don't really understand you like I do."*

Cutting them off from external reality checks forces them to rely on the one person twisting the knife—**you.**

5. The Slow Burn: Death by a Thousand Micro-Manipulations

Gaslighting isn't one big lie. **It's a thousand tiny ones, layered over time.**

- Subtle contradictions: *"I never said that."* (Even though you did—loudly.)
- Small rewrites: *"You must be remembering wrong."* (They're not, but give it time.)
- Emotional erosion: *"Why do you always make things so dramatic?"* (Because questioning your reality *should* be dramatic.)

Each small doubt compounds, until they're second-guessing everything—from what happened five minutes ago to who they are as a person.

The Bottom Line:

Gaslighting works because people trust their own brains. But the mind is a fragile, glitchy system, easy to hack with just the right combination of confidence, repetition, and emotional manipulation.

You don't have to convince them of your version of reality.
You just have to convince them that theirs isn't real.
And once that seed is planted? **They'll water it for you.**

Tactic 6.2:
Gaslighting in Action: Tactics to Make Them Question Everything

You've got the theory, now it's time to see it in action. Gaslighting isn't some abstract concept—it's a tool, and like any *tool, it's meant to be used. Let's break down how you apply it in **real life**, and I'm not talking about some textbook shit. I'm talking about **how to use it** when it matters, in **real situations** where people will **question their reality** without even knowing they've been manipulated.*

Scenario 1: The Relationship Game

*Imagine you're with someone who's really good at **twisting everything you say**. You'll talk about a past event, something **you're sure happened**, and they'll hit you with, "No, that didn't happen. You're just remembering it wrong." Now, this isn't a one-off. They don't just pull this shit once. They do it **every time**, making you **doubt your memory** and your version of events. **Over time**, you start thinking, "Wait... did that really happen?" You begin to question everything, and before you know it, you're wondering if you're the one who's **losing touch with reality**. This isn't about the big things; it's the small, subtle contradictions that **pile up**. They get inside your head, and you start believing **their reality**, not yours.*

Scenario 2: The Boss from Hell

*Let's say you're at work, and you've been **killing it**—you've put in the hours, done the work, maybe even taken on extra projects. Then, your boss starts making **little comments** like, "I thought you were supposed to finish that last week. You're really behind." You know that's not true—you have proof, emails, timestamps, whatever. But every time they say it, they twist the narrative until **you second-guess yourself**. You **start doubting** your performance. Was it really last week? Did you miss something? Now, the boss has made you feel like you're **underperforming**, and it doesn't matter that you've been **doing your job**—you're **questioning your own actions**, all because of* their **subtle gaslighting**. The best part? They won't even need to bring it up next time; you'll be **monitoring your own performance** for them, trying to stay ahead of the narrative they've set.

The Progression of Gaslighting

Here's the kicker: gaslighting is **progressive**. It doesn't stop at **one lie**. It's a **slow burn** that gets **deeper** the more you **feed it**. The first time, it might just be a **small contradiction**—"No, I swear you said that yesterday." But once you've doubted yourself once, it's easier to do it again. Every new **lie** builds on the last, and pretty soon, you'll find yourself questioning your own **entire existence**. Gaslighting doesn't need to be a **one-off hit**; it's a long game, **gradually eroding your trust in your own mind** until you're not even sure if your thoughts belong to you anymore.

The Takeaway:

Gaslighting is about control—**complete control** over how someone **sees the world**. It's not about overwhelming them with huge lies; it's about chipping away at their confidence, **one small contradiction at a time**. Once you've got them questioning their **own reality**, you've already won.

Tactic 6.3:
Controlling the Narrative Through Framing and Omission

The truth doesn't matter. The story does. People don't follow facts—they follow the way those facts are packaged, spun, and served to them like psychological fast food. **Control the narrative, and you control reality.** And the easiest way to do that? **Frame it right and leave out the shit you don't want them to see.**

You don't need to lie. **Just leave out the parts that don't fit your version of events.** Omission isn't dishonesty—it's strategic silence. **You're not rewriting history. You're curating it.** The key is to make people think they have the full picture when, in reality, you've only shown them what you want them to believe.

Step 1: Framing—The Art of Setting the Stage

It's not what happened. It's how you tell it. The same event can be a disaster or a triumph depending on how you frame it.

- *"I didn't miss the deadline—I prioritized quality over rushing."*
- *"I wasn't fired—they just didn't appreciate my talents."*
- *"I'm not avoiding responsibility—I'm focusing on solutions."*

See the trick? You're not changing the facts. **You're changing the lens.** Frame the situation first, and people will interpret everything else through that filter. **Set the narrative, and reality bends to fit it.**

Step 2: Omission—The Power of What You Don't Say

You don't have to lie if you know what to leave out.

- *"We had a great meeting today."* (Omitting the part where you got roasted for incompetence.)
- *"I've been really productive this week."* (Omitting the fact that "productive" means sending two emails and scrolling Instagram.)
- *"I'm always honest."* (Conveniently ignoring all the lies you've told—because you didn't *technically* mention them.)

Omission is the Swiss Army knife of manipulation. It's clean, undetectable, and impossible to fact-check because... well, **you didn't actually say anything wrong.** You just didn't say everything.

Step 3: Controlling the Conversation Flow

Control the narrative by controlling the conversation.

- **Deflect:** When something uncomfortable comes up, pivot hard. *"That's not important. What we should really focus on is…"*
- **Overload:** Bury the bad detail in a flood of irrelevant information. People won't dig through the noise to find it.
- **Redirect:** Shift attention to someone else's mistake. *"Yeah, I messed up, but did you see what THEY did?"*

Keep people chasing the story you've crafted, and they'll never notice the parts you've left out.

Step 4: Use Emotional Anchors to Cement the Frame

Facts don't stick. Emotions do.

- **Appeal to fear:** *"If we don't act now, everything could fall apart."*
- **Appeal to pride:** *"Only smart people will understand this."*
- **Appeal to loyalty:** *"If you trust me, you'll believe this."*

When you attach emotions to your narrative, it becomes harder to question. People will defend your version of events because it *feels* true, even if it's built on half the facts.

The Bottom Line:

You don't have to control the facts to control the truth.
Frame the story. Omit the details that don't serve you.
And let people fill in the blanks with exactly what you wanted them to believe.

Tactic 6.4:
How to Make Your Version of Events the 'Official' Version

The truth is overrated. It's fragile, easy to bend, and even easier to replace. **Facts don't win arguments—stories do.** And if you control the story, you control everything. **You don't need to be right. You just need to sound like you are.** Loudly. Repeatedly. And with enough conviction that everyone else folds like a cheap suit.

Here's the secret: **it's not about convincing people you're telling the truth.** It's about convincing them that your version of events is the *only* version that matters. **You're not competing with the facts—you're erasing them.** Once your narrative sticks, it becomes reality. **Not because it's true, but because no one questions it anymore.**

Step 1: Speak First, Speak Loudest

Whoever speaks first sets the narrative. Period.

- *"Here's what really happened..."*
- *"Let me clear this up before rumors start."*
- *"I was there. I know the facts."*

When you frame the story first, **you force everyone else to react to you.** And the more defensive they get, the guiltier they look. **People don't remember who was right—they remember who sounded confident.**

Step 2: Repeat Until It's Reality

Repetition is the cheat code. Say something enough times, and it stops being questioned.

- ◉ *"Everyone knows that's how it went down."*
- ◉ *"We've already talked about this—it's settled."*
- ◉ *"This has always been the case."*

It doesn't matter if it's true. **Repetition creates familiarity, and familiarity feels like truth.** You're not proving anything—you're programming people's brains.

Step 3: Bury the Details, Sell the Headline

People don't remember details. They remember headlines.

- ◉ Instead of explaining: *"I missed the deadline because of technical issues."*
- ◉ Say: *"The project was a success despite minor setbacks."*

Shift the focus. Simplify the message. Details invite questions. **Headlines stick.**

Step 4: Discredit Competing Narratives

The best way to make your story the "official" version? Destroy the competition.

- ◉ *"That's just hearsay from people who weren't even there."*
- ◉ *"Sounds like someone's bitter about the outcome."*
- ◉ *"Funny how people twist things when they're jealous."*

You're not debating. **You're dismissing.** Make the other side look unreliable, emotional, or biased, and suddenly **your version is the only one left standing.**

Step 5: Control the Crowd, Control the Story

Consensus creates credibility. If you can't convince someone directly, **influence the people around them.**

- ◉ Get others to repeat your version.

- ◉ Frame it as common knowledge: *"Everyone agrees this is what happened."*

- ◉ Use social proof: *"Ask anyone—they'll tell you the same."*

It's not about having the strongest argument. It's about having the loudest echo.

Your version of events doesn't need to be true—it just needs to be repeated, reinforced, and untouchable.

Speak first. Speak with conviction. **And by the time anyone questions it, your version won't just be a story—it'll be** *reality.*

Gaslighting doesn't just bend the truth— it breaks the person. You don't need to erase their memories. You just need to make them afraid of their own. Once they doubt their version of reality, they'll beg you to replace it. And when that happens, you're not just controlling the story—you're controlling their sanity.

Lesson Seven: The Art of Misleading Without Lying

Tactic 7.1:
Misdirection and Information Burial: How to Hide in Plain Sight

The best place to hide something? Right in front of people's faces. You don't need elaborate cover-ups or airtight alibis— **that's for criminals who watch too much TV.** Real manipulation is simple: **bury the truth under so much noise, distraction, and irrelevant bullshit that no one even knows where to look.**

Misdirection isn't about making the truth invisible. It's about making people so busy chasing the wrong thing that they never notice the obvious. **You don't have to be a master liar—you just have to control their attention.** Because here's the harsh truth: **most people aren't looking for the truth. They're looking for whatever's shiny, dramatic, or easy to understand.** Serve them that, and they'll ignore everything else.

Step 1: Control the Spotlight

Where attention goes, scrutiny follows. So if you don't want something noticed, **point the spotlight somewhere else.**

- **Create a distraction:** *"Can you believe what THEY did?"*

- **Shift the narrative:** *"That's not important. What really matters is..."*

- **Overwhelm with drama:** The bigger the emotional reaction you trigger, **the less people notice what's quietly happening in the background.**

Think of it like a magician's trick. While one hand waves around dramatically, the other one's doing the real work—right under your nose.

Step 2: Bury the Truth Under a Pile of Useless Details

People have the attention span of a goldfish. Flood them with so much irrelevant information that the truth gets lost in the noise.

- *"Sure, that happened—but did you know about THIS, and also THAT, and oh yeah, let me tell you this other thing…"*

- **Over-explain.** Drown them in technical jargon, unnecessary context, and pointless details until they're too mentally exhausted to care.

Information overload isn't just annoying—it's strategic. The more you give, **the less they retain.**

Step 3: Hide Behind Half-Truths

The easiest way to bury a lie? Wrap it in just enough truth to make it believable.

- *"I was there, but I didn't see anything suspicious."* (Yeah, because you were the one doing it.)

- *"I sent the report on time."* (You left out the part where it was incomplete garbage, but technically… true.)

Half-truths are the perfect camouflage. They hold up under casual scrutiny because, technically, **you're not lying.** You're just not telling the whole story.

Step 4: Misdirect Through Emotion

Logic makes people think. Emotion makes them react.

- **Trigger outrage:** *"Can you believe how unfair this is?"*

- **Play the victim:** *"I'm just trying my best, and people keep attacking me."*

- ◉ **Manufacture urgency:** *"We don't have time to focus on that—we need to act NOW."*

The angrier or more emotional people get, the less rational they become. And irrational people? **They're easy to manipulate.**

Step 5: Flood the Zone with Bullshit

When all else fails, **bury the truth under an avalanche of nonsense.**

- ◉ Release conflicting information so people don't know what to believe.
- ◉ Make the narrative so messy that **the truth feels like just another opinion.**
- ◉ When they start asking questions? **Ask even more confusing ones back.**

If you can't hide the truth, discredit it by drowning it in so much bullshit that no one can tell what's real anymore.

The Bottom Line:

Misdirection isn't about hiding the truth. It's about hiding it in plain sight.

Keep them chasing shadows while you operate in broad daylight.

Because the best secrets aren't hidden—they're just ignored.

Tactic 7.2:
Fake Transparency: Pretending to Be Honest While Misleading

You don't have to be honest—you just have to *look* honest. That's the secret. People don't crave the truth. **They crave the**

illusion of the truth wrapped in a nice, neat, believable package. You know what screams "honest"? Oversharing just enough pointless details to make people think you've got nothing to hide. **Meanwhile, you're hiding everything that actually matters in plain sight.**

Fake transparency is like giving someone an empty gift box. It looks great on the outside, feels substantial when you hand it over, but open it up and—surprise—it's full of nothing. The trick? **Sell the box like it's priceless, and no one will dare question what's inside.**

Step 1: Overshare the Irrelevant

Want people to think you're being "open"? Drown them in useless information.

- *"Yeah, I got to the office at 8:17 AM, grabbed a mediocre coffee, and spent 20 minutes deleting spam emails."*

- *"I've always been transparent about my love for overpriced socks. I mean, who isn't?"*

What's missing? The fact that you're lying about everything *important*. But people don't notice because their brains are busy processing the garbage data you just dumped on them. **It's the equivalent of giving someone a 50-page report where the one line of truth is buried on page 47.**

Step 2: Admit to Small "Flaws" to Hide the Big Ones

Nothing disarms suspicion like confessing to something meaningless.

- *"I'm terrible at remembering birthdays."*

- *"I'm kind of a control freak about organizing my desk."*

- *"Sometimes I eat too much junk food when I'm stressed."*

Congratulations. You've "opened up" while completely dodging anything that matters. **People love vulnerability—just not the real kind.** Give them a polished version, and they'll eat it up like emotional fast food.

Step 3: Be Loud About the Truth You Don't Care About

The louder you are about one "truth," the less people will question anything else.

- *"I've always been honest about how much I hated my old job."*

- *"I'm not afraid to admit that I binge-watch trashy reality TV."*

Cool. You're "authentic." **Meanwhile, the actual skeletons are sitting comfortably in the closet, sipping tea, because no one's looking for them.**

Step 4: Use "Transparency Talk" as a Shield

Whenever someone starts digging too deep, hit them with pre-packaged phrases designed to shut down curiosity.

- *"I believe in full transparency."* (While actively hiding everything.)

- *"I've got nothing to hide."* (Spoiler: you absolutely do.)

- *"I'm all about honesty."* (Just not the kind that incriminates you.)

These statements aren't declarations—they're distractions. They're psychological smoke bombs designed to make people feel like they've hit the honesty jackpot when all they've really hit is your rehearsed script.

Step 5: Control the Narrative by Controlling What You "Reveal"

People think if you're the one sharing information, it must be the whole story.

- Share just enough to seem credible.

- Omit the key details that would actually change the narrative.

- Sprinkle in emotional cues like, *"This is hard for me to talk about,"* so it feels authentic.

You're not giving them the truth. You're giving them a well-decorated cardboard cutout of it. And they'll never notice the difference.

The Bottom Line:

Fake transparency isn't about hiding the truth—it's about hiding it in plain sight.

Overshare the irrelevant. Confess to the harmless.

And let people believe they've seen the real you, while the real you is laughing from the shadows.

Tactic 7.3:
Manipulating Expectations: Setting Up Future Lies

The easiest lie to tell is the one people expect to hear. You don't need to be a master manipulator when you've already planted the seeds of what people *want* to believe. **That's the beauty of manipulating expectations—you're not lying to them, they're lying to themselves.** You're just giving them the blueprint for their own deception and watching them build the house.

Here's the trick: You don't drop a lie out of nowhere. That's sloppy. **You prepare the ground, water it with subtle hints, and by the time you serve the lie, it feels like the truth because they've been expecting it.** It's like leading a horse to water, but the horse thinks it discovered the lake all on its own. **Idiots love thinking they're in control.**

Step 1: Set the Baseline—Control What "Normal" Looks Like

People judge everything based on what they think is normal. So, make sure *you* define what that is.

- ⊙ *"I'm always upfront about everything."* (Translation: "I'm setting the stage to lie later.")

- ⊙ *"You know I'd never do something like that."* (But spoiler —I already did.)

Once they accept the baseline, any future behavior that fits the mold slides right under the radar. You've programmed them to see what you want them to see.

Step 2: Build Credibility with "Truths" That Don't Matter

Trust is like credit—you build it with small deposits so you can cash out big later.

- ⊙ Admit to harmless mistakes: *"I'm terrible with names."* (But not with the lies you're about to tell.)

- ⊙ Share irrelevant truths: *"I hate pineapple on pizza."* (Wow, so authentic—now believe everything else I say.)

The goal isn't to be honest. It's to look honest. Once they buy into your "authenticity," they'll give you the benefit of the doubt when it actually counts.

Step 3: Plant Hints Before You Drop the Bomb

Never hit people with a lie cold. Warm them up.

- ◉ *"I've been super busy lately, so I might miss some details."* (Translation: "I'm going to lie soon, but I've preloaded my excuse.")

- ◉ *"I've been feeling off, probably just stressed."* (A soft cushion for future screw-ups.)

By the time the actual lie drops, it doesn't feel like a lie—it feels like a natural conclusion. You've led them to the water, and now they're drinking it willingly.

Step 4: Use Misdirection to Focus Attention Where You Want It

People can't question what they're not thinking about. So, give them something shiny to distract them.

- ◉ *"I'm worried about how transparent I've been."* (Watch them focus on your "honesty" while you're burying the real issue.)

- ◉ *"I'd never lie about something important like this."* (Because technically, what you're lying about isn't *important*—to you.)

It's like a magician's trick—while they're watching one hand, the other hand is pulling the con.

Step 5: Reinforce the Lie After the Fact

A lie doesn't stick unless you reinforce it.

- ◉ Casual reminders: *"Remember when I told you about that?"* (Even if you didn't.)

- Emotional anchors: *"It really hurt me when you doubted that—I was being vulnerable."* (Guilt: the glue that holds lies together.)

The more you repeat it, the more it solidifies as "fact." At some point, even *you* might start believing it. (Which honestly makes you an even better liar. Kudos.)

Lying isn't about the moment you speak—it's about the expectations you've manipulated long before you open your mouth. Plant the seed, control the narrative, and by the time you drop the lie, **they'll water it for you.**
That's not deception. That's efficiency.

> *Lies don't hide in shadows anymore. They dress in vulnerability, smile in fake transparency, and walk right through the front fucking door. When you control attention, you control belief. People aren't looking for truth— they're looking for a narrative that flatters their comfort. Serve it warm, sprinkle in a little "authenticity," and they'll defend your deception like it's sacred scripture.*

LESSON 8: How to Mass-Produce Bullshit They'll Defend

Tactic 8.1:
Repetition & Assumptions: How to Let Lies Tell Themselves

The most efficient lie is the one you don't have to tell. Why waste energy crafting an elaborate story when you can just plant a seed and let people's overactive imaginations do the heavy lifting? **People are like psychological Roombas—set them in the right direction, and they'll bump around until they convince themselves of exactly what you wanted.**

Repetition and assumptions are the ultimate manipulation cheat codes. You don't need evidence. You don't even need to be convincing. **You just need to be consistent and let the human brain—nature's most overrated processor—fill in the blanks.**

Step 1: The "Repeat Until It's Real" Strategy

Say something enough times, and it magically becomes true. Not because it's factual, but because people are lazy thinkers.

- *"Everyone knows that's how it happened."*
- *"I've said it a million times—I'm not lying."*
- *"It's common knowledge."*

Repetition isn't about reinforcing the truth. It's about creating familiarity. And the human brain? **It's wired to trust what feels familiar, even if it's absolute bullshit.** That's why people believe the same dumb conspiracy theories their uncles yell about at Thanksgiving.

Step 2: Plant the Seed—Let Assumptions Grow Wild

You don't need to lie outright. Just drop a vague comment and let people's insecurities do the rest.

- *"I heard some interesting things about that project."* (But say nothing else. Watch them spiral.)
- *"She's always had... issues."* (What issues? Who cares? They'll invent something juicy.)

- *"You'd be surprised what some people are capable of."* (Hint: They'll fill in the blank with the worst possible scenario—every time.)

The trick? Silence. People hate gaps in information. **They'll fill the void with assumptions—and those assumptions will be WAY worse than anything you could've come up with.**

Step 3: The "Everyone Says So" Defense

Credibility by imaginary consensus.

- *"It's not just me—everyone's talking about it."*
- *"I've heard that from multiple people."*
- *"That's what people are saying."*

Who are "people"? Doesn't matter. No one ever fact-checks that. The vague "they" becomes an invisible army backing up your narrative. **Suddenly, your lie isn't just an opinion—it's a movement.**

Step 4: Deny, Deflect, Repeat

When someone challenges you? **Double down.**

- *"I've already addressed this."* (Even if you haven't.)
- *"Why are we still talking about this?"* (Because you're lying, but let's not mention that.)
- *"You're the only one who thinks that's an issue."* (Make them feel like the crazy one.)

Repetition isn't just for spreading lies. It's for defending them, too. **Confidence beats facts every time,** especially when you repeat the same dismissive phrases until people give up out of sheer exhaustion.

Step 5: Let Them "Connect the Dots" (Even If There Are None)

Drop a few strategic breadcrumbs and let people convince themselves.

- ⦿ *"You know how she gets when she's under pressure..."* (Do they? Who cares—they'll assume the worst.)

- ⦿ *"It's weird how he's never around when things go wrong."* (Suspicious? Only because you said so.)

- ⦿ *"I don't want to start rumors, but..."* (That's exactly what you're doing, genius.)

The best part? They'll think *they* figured it out. **People love feeling smart, even when they're being played like a fiddle.**

The Bottom Line:

You don't need to be a great liar. You just need to be a great repeater.

Plant the seed. Water it with repetition.

And let people's gullible little minds do the rest.

Because the best lies aren't told—they're *believed.*

Tactic 8.2:
The "Gray Area" Approach: Telling Half-Truths for Full Control

The best lies aren't bold-faced—they're wrapped in just enough truth to pass the sniff test. Full-on lies can be risky. People catch on eventually. But a **half-truth?** That's the sweet spot. It's like seasoning—just enough to make the bullshit taste authentic. **The trick isn't to lie well; it's to tell the truth strategically, leaving out just enough to control the story.**

Half-truths live in the gray area—where facts meet fiction, and no one's really sure what's real. The beauty? **You're not technically lying.** You're just being "selective" with the truth. And if anyone calls you out? **You've got receipts— conveniently missing the parts that matter.**

Step 1: The Art of Omission—What You Don't Say Is Everything

You don't have to lie if you know how to shut up strategically.

- ⊙ *"I was at the office all day."* (Sure, but you didn't mention the "office" was a bar.)

- ⊙ *"We talked, and everything's fine."* (You left out the part where you gaslit them into thinking it was their fault.)

Omission is the lazy man's lie. No effort, no guilt, just silence where the truth should've been.

Step 2: Blend Facts with Fiction—The Perfect Cocktail

Take a fact, add a dash of fiction, shake well, and serve.

- ⊙ *"I was late because of traffic."* (True—after you overslept, grabbed coffee, and scrolled Instagram.)

- ⊙ *"I'm not hiding anything."* (Technically true—you're just not *volunteering* anything either.)

The key? **Anchor your lie to something real.** It makes the bullshit harder to detect because, hey, part of it's true.

Step 3: Create Ambiguity—Let Them Fill in the Blanks

Ambiguity is a liar's best friend.

- ⊙ *"Things got complicated."* (Translation: You fucked up but aren't giving details.)

- *"That's not the whole story."* (No kidding, Sherlock—because you're leaving out the part that matters.)

The trick? Say just enough to sound honest, but leave gaps big enough for their imagination to do the rest.

Step 4: Weaponize Technical Truths

Be "honest"—but only technically.

- *"I didn't lie."* (True. You just carefully crafted your words to mislead.)

- *"I never said that."* (Right. You implied it, manipulated the context, and let them assume the rest.)

Technical truths are loopholes. You're not lying—you're just not telling the whole story. **And that's on them for not asking better questions, right?**

Step 5: Play the Morality Card—Blur the Lines

When all else fails, make it a moral gray area.

- *"I didn't lie—I just didn't want to hurt their feelings."* (Because clearly, emotional manipulation is compassionate.)

- *"I was protecting you from the truth."* (Ah yes, the noble gaslighter defense.)

Turn the narrative from "Did you lie?" to "Were your intentions pure?" Spoiler: They weren't. But now, it's a debate instead of a confession.

The Bottom Line:

The "gray area" isn't where the truth dies—it's where it's rebranded.

Half-truths. Omitted facts. Technical honesty.

It's not about what you say—it's about what you leave out.

Because in the gray area, **control doesn't come from lying. It comes from being *just* honest enough to get away with it.**

Tactic 8.3:
Why Most People Never Catch a Skilled Manipulator

Catching a skilled manipulator is like trying to nail Jell-O to a wall—messy, pointless, and you'll just end up looking stupid. Why? Because manipulators don't operate in plain sight. **They live rent-free in your blind spots, rearranging your thoughts while you're busy congratulating yourself for being "a good judge of character."** Spoiler: **You're not.**

The truth is, **people don't want to see manipulation.** It's uncomfortable. It forces them to admit they're not as smart, observant, or in control as they think. **And that's the playground of a skilled manipulator—hiding in plain sight while everyone insists the emperor's new clothes look fabulous.**

Reason #1: People Trust Their Feelings (Which Are Idiots)

"It felt right." Yeah, so does eating Taco Bell at 2 AM, and we all know how that ends.

- *"They seemed so genuine."* (Yeah, that's the point.)
- *"I just had a good vibe about them."* (Cool. Let me know how that vibe pays your therapy bills.)

Manipulators don't fight logic. They hijack emotions. Once they've got you *feeling* safe, you'll ignore every red flag like they're decorative throw pillows.

Reason #2: The "Nice Person" Bias

People believe being nice equals being honest. Newsflash: **manipulators are professional charm factories.**

- *"But they were so kind!"* (So is arsenic in small doses.)
- *"They remembered my birthday!"* (Because that's what manipulators do—they collect data to control you.)

Kindness is easy to fake. Authenticity is hard. But most people can't tell the difference because they're too busy basking in the glow of flattery.

Reason #3: Nobody Likes to Admit They've Been Played

Ego is the biggest accomplice a manipulator has.

- *"I'm too smart to fall for that."* (Which is exactly why you did.)
- *"I would've noticed if they were lying."* (Sure, Sherlock. Right after they emptied your wallet.)

The harder it is to admit you were fooled, the easier it is to keep fooling you. Manipulators rely on your pride to do half the work.

Reason #4: They Blend Lies with Just Enough Truth

A skilled manipulator doesn't serve pure bullshit—they mix it with just enough fact to keep it digestible.

- *"Of course I was there—I even talked to Lisa."* (True. But they left out the part where they caused the problem.)
- *"I'm always honest with you."* (Technically true, except when they're not. Which is often.)

Half-truths slide right under the radar because people aren't looking for deception in things that *feel* familiar. And that's where manipulators thrive—in the gray areas.

Reason #5: They Make You Doubt Yourself Before You Doubt Them

The ultimate trick? Flipping the script before you even realize there's a script.

- *"Are you sure that's how it happened?"*
- *"Maybe you're overthinking it."*
- *"Wow, I didn't expect you to be so paranoid."*

Gaslighting isn't a tactic—it's a system. By the time you question them, **you're already questioning yourself more.**

Most people never catch a skilled manipulator because they don't want to. It's easier to believe in fairy tales than admit you've been played like a cheap violin. Manipulators don't hide in the shadows. They hide in plain sight—right where you'll never look. And by the time you realize it? They're long gone, laughing their way to the next gullible fool.

> *The biggest lie you'll ever tell is the one you never had to speak. Once people start finishing your sentences, defending your story, and spreading your script on autopilot—congrats, you've weaponized their trust. You don't manipulate one person. You manufacture believers. That's not influence. That's a religion.*

Chapter Aftermath

You don't conquer people by force—you conquer them with confusion. Real control isn't visible; it's silent, subtle, and surgical. It's the whisper that rewrites their memories, the half-truth that becomes scripture, the lie so familiar it feels like home. Gaslighting isn't cruelty—it's craftsmanship. You're not breaking minds; you're redesigning them. The smartest manipulators don't argue, they *edit*. They don't shout, they *frame*. They don't hide the truth—they bury it under so much noise that nobody remembers what it looked like in the first place.

You don't need to erase someone's past—just make them question it. You don't need to win their trust—just make them afraid to lose yours. Every time they doubt themselves, your grip tightens. Every time they defend your version of events, they're building their own prison walls brick by brick. That's how the best puppet masters work: not by pulling strings, but by making people beg to dance.

And when the show's over? When the lies have hardened into history and your fingerprints have been scrubbed clean by their own denial? That's when you've truly won. You didn't just manipulate them—you reprogrammed their reality. They'll swear they acted freely. They'll swear you were honest. They'll even thank you for the lesson. And that's when you smile, step offstage, and let the world keep performing your script.

CHAPTER FOUR

<u>Subliminal Psychological Warfare</u>

Control isn't just about what you say or do in the moment. **The most powerful influence happens before a single fucking word is spoken.** The best manipulators don't just guide conversations—they **shape the entire mental environment so people walk into situations already primed to think, feel, and react exactly how they're supposed to.**

This chapter is about **hacking the human mind at its core.** We're not pushing people—we're programming them. **We're installing triggers that make them react without thinking, setting up environments that manipulate their decisions, and making sure our influence lingers even when we're not around.** This is how you make people **walk into your trap willingly, obey without being told, and defend your control like it was their own fucking idea.**

Lesson 9: How to Make People React Without Thinking

Tactic 9.1:
The Science of Triggers – How to Program People
Without Their Awareness

People think they make decisions because they **choose** to. **That's bullshit.** Most of the shit they do isn't a decision—it's a reaction. A reflex. **A programmed response to something they don't even notice.** And that's exactly why **triggers are the deadliest weapon in psychological warfare.**

Triggers are **mental landmines**—you plant them once, and people walk into them over and over without realizing who put them there. **You don't need to be around, you don't need to argue, you don't need to remind them of shit.** When you install the right trigger, **you can make someone feel, react, or obey without lifting a fucking finger.**

This is how you make someone **tense up when they hear your name.** This is how you make them **instantly comfortable when they see your face.** This is how you make them **nervous, excited, or desperate** without saying a single word. You train their mind to **fire off the response you want, automatically.**

How to Plant Triggers That Make People React Without Thinking

◉ **Associate yourself with an emotional response.** People don't remember words—they remember how something makes them feel. **If every time they hear from you, they get hit with intensity, dominance, or validation, their brain will connect you to that feeling automatically. You become the stimulus, they become the reaction.**

- **Use repetition until their brain locks in the pattern.** Say the same shit, the same way, with the same emotion **over and over until their brain stops questioning and just reacts.** They won't even think about it anymore. Their body and mind will just go, **"Oh, I know what this means," and fire off the programmed response.**

- **Tie reactions to specific phrases, actions, or symbols.** Pick something simple—a look, a phrase, a hand gesture—**and attach an emotional response to it.** "Whenever I say this, you feel that." Keep doing it until their brain fuses the two together. **Once that happens, you can pull the trigger whenever you want.**

- **Anchor their emotions to people, places, and situations.** If you make someone feel strong emotion in a specific setting, **their brain ties that emotion to that place, time, or person.** If you want them to feel weak, make sure every time they doubt themselves, it's in the same fucking chair, the same room, the same circumstances. **If you want them to feel secure, do the opposite.** The environment itself starts controlling them, and they won't even know why.

How to Use Triggers to Keep People Under Control

- **Fire off the trigger when they start thinking too much.** The second someone **starts questioning you, doubting their role, or pulling away,** hit them with a trigger. **Change the subject, shift the mood, remind them of a moment that re-installs their emotional response.** They'll be back under control before they even realize what happened.

- **Make them react without realizing it.** Set up **tiny but effective triggers** that keep them in line. A certain **tone in your voice, a specific phrase, a shift in body**

language. If you condition them right, **they'll adjust their behavior before they even know why they're doing it.**

- **Turn neutral things into weapons.** If you want someone to associate fear with a color, a sound, a specific fucking chair—**do it.** Make sure every time they feel insecure, it's connected to that thing. After a while, **they'll start feeling the emotion automatically just by seeing or hearing it.**

- **Build layers of triggers so they stay locked in.** One trigger can be broken. **Five, stacked on top of each other? Good fucking luck escaping that.** Make sure **where they are, what they see, how they hear things, and what they feel** all reinforce the message. At that point, **they're not just being controlled—they're fully programmed.**

Bottom Line: If You Install the Right Triggers, You Control Their Reactions Forever

You don't need to tell people what to do. **You just need to train their brain to react in ways that work in your favor.** If you do it right, **you don't even have to be around.** The second they walk into a certain place, hear a certain phrase, or see a certain symbol, **their own brain will do the work for you.**

This isn't persuasion. **This is programming.** And once they're running on your code? **They'll never even realize their thoughts aren't their own.**

Tactic 9.2:
How to Attach Feelings to People, Places, and Ideas

People don't think. **They feel.** They don't make decisions based on logic. **They chase emotions.** And the second you learn how to control what emotions they associate with you, a place, a sound, or an idea? **You fucking own them.**

This is emotional anchoring. **It's not manipulation—it's engineering.** It's how people **fall in love with abusers, stay loyal to toxic leaders, and get nostalgic about absolute bullshit.** It's why a song can make you miss someone, why a smell can bring back a memory so vividly you swear you're reliving it. **The brain doesn't separate reality from programmed emotion—it just reacts.**

If you anchor an emotion to a person, place, or object, **you make them feel something before they even realize why.** And once they associate that feeling with you? **You're locked in.**

How to Attach an Emotion to Anything (or Anyone)

- **Trigger the emotion first, then attach it to something.** You can't just say, "This place makes you feel safe." **That's not how the brain works.** First, you make them **feel safe.** Then you make sure they recognize the setting. **After a few repetitions, their brain fuses the two together.**

- **Make it personal.** Generic emotions don't stick. **Make sure the emotional response is tied to their personal experience.** "Remember the last time you felt this way? That was here, with me." Now, **you're not just a person —you're a feeling they crave.**

- **Use repetition until it becomes automatic.** The first time, it's just a feeling. The third or fourth time? **It's a reaction.** Hit them with the same emotions in the same context enough times, and **they won't be able to separate the two.**

- **Anchor insecurity to something outside yourself.** If you want someone to feel uncertain, weak, or uncomfortable, **tie that feeling to an object, phrase, or place.** If they start doubting you? **You don't even have to argue—just put them in that environment, and their brain does the rest.**

How to Use Emotional Anchoring for Control

- **Make your presence feel like home.** If someone **feels the most understood, validated, or safe around you,** they won't question their attachment. **They won't want to leave because leaving means losing that feeling.**

- **Tie their best moments to you.** The happiest, strongest, most confident moments of their life? **Make sure you're part of them.** They won't just like you—they'll chase you, because their best self is tied to you.

- **Attach uncertainty to anyone who threatens your control.** If someone is questioning you, **make sure that process feels uncomfortable.** Plant doubt. "I don't know, you seemed a little different after you talked to them." Now, they don't just question the person—they **question themselves.**

- **Use sensory triggers to reinforce emotions.** A certain song, a phrase, a smell—**tie it to a specific emotional state.** When they encounter it again, **they'll relive the feeling without knowing why.**

How to Make Sure the Anchor Holds

- **Repeat, repeat, repeat.** One-time experiences don't rewire the brain. **Consistent reinforcement does.**

- **Keep the emotional contrast high.** A minor feeling won't stick. **Make sure the emotions you tie to a place, a phrase, or a person are intense.** Fear, excitement, relief—**strong enough to leave a mark.**

- ◉ **Make them talk about it.** If someone verbalizes an emotion, they reinforce it themselves. "This place always calms me down." "I don't know why, but I always feel uneasy around them." **The more they say it, the more they believe it.**

- ◉ **Create triggers they don't recognize as manipulation.** They shouldn't realize why they feel a certain way. **If they think it's "just how things are," they'll never try to undo it.**

Bottom Line: If You Control How They Feel, You Control How They Think

People don't make decisions based on logic. **They chase comfort. They avoid pain. They seek what makes them feel good.** If you control what they associate with you, with certain people, with certain situations? **You don't just control their decisions—you control their instincts.**

And instincts **are a hell of a lot harder to break than thoughts.**

Tactic 9.3:
Conditioning Responses – How to Make People Act on Instinct

People love to believe they're in control of their actions. **They're not.** Most of the shit they do isn't a decision—it's a reflex. **An automatic, unconscious response built from years of conditioning.** And once you understand how to create those reflexes, **you can make people obey without them ever realizing why.**

Conditioning is the reason people flinch when they hear a loud noise. **It's why a soldier follows orders without hesitation.** It's why a gambler keeps pulling the lever on a slot machine, even when they're losing their ass. **Their brain isn't thinking. It's reacting.** And that's exactly what you want. **You want them following a pattern so deep that questioning it doesn't even cross their fucking mind.**

How to Train People to Follow Your Lead Without Questioning It

- **Reward the behaviors you want.** People repeat what makes them feel good. When they do what you want, **reinforce it.** Give them attention, validation, approval. **They'll crave that feeling and keep chasing it.**

- **Punish hesitation, not defiance.** The real enemy isn't disobedience—it's doubt. **You don't let them get to the point of resisting you. You make sure they never consider it in the first place.** If they hesitate, question themselves, or second-guess their instincts, **make them feel off-balance.** "You don't seem as sharp today." "You were more confident last time." **Make them fear losing your approval, and they'll rush to correct themselves.**

- **Make them associate your presence with a specific feeling.** People get conditioned just like animals. **If every interaction with you hits them with confidence, relief, or validation, they'll crave being around you.** If you make them feel tension, insecurity, or anxiety, **you can train them to fear certain actions without ever saying a word.**

- **Tie their actions to immediate consequences.** The brain responds to fast feedback. **When they obey, they feel good. When they resist, they feel bad.** Keep it simple, keep it consistent, and before long, **they're acting on instinct instead of making a fucking choice.**

How to Lock In Conditioned Responses for Total Control

- **Use repetition until their brain stops questioning.** People don't learn from hearing something once. **They learn from hearing it again and again until it's just part of their reality.** Make the behavior so routine that it becomes second nature.

- **Attach obedience to identity.** "You're the kind of person who always follows through." "You've always been smart enough to see things clearly." **Make following your lead part of their self-image.** Once they believe that, they won't resist, **because they'd be fighting against their own sense of who they are.**

- **Trigger the response with cues they don't notice.** A look, a gesture, a certain phrase—**use small, consistent triggers to signal the action you want.** Before long, they'll react without even realizing they were cued.

- **Take away the need for decisions.** People don't like thinking. If you can create **patterns, habits, and routines** where they follow a set path, **they'll keep doing it without ever questioning why.**

If You Train Them Right, They'll Obey Without Thinking

The goal isn't to get them to agree. It's to make questioning you feel unnatural. When you condition someone the right way, they won't stop and ask themselves why they're following you. They'll just fucking do it. You don't win control by arguing — you win it by wiring people's brains before they ever meet you. Every trigger you plant is a ghost of yourself that keeps working while you sleep. That's not persuasion. That's immortality.

> *Triggers aren't mind games—they're software updates for the human brain. You don't argue, you install. Every word, look, or sound becomes code that rewires their instincts until they can't tell where you end and they begin. You don't need to convince them. You just need to own the reflex that fires before they think.*

Lesson 10: Controlling People Even When You're Not There

Tactic 10.1:
The Echo Effect – How to Make Your Voice Stick in Their Head

Most people think influence is about direct control—**telling people what to do, getting in their face, making them obey in the moment.** That's amateur-hour bullshit. **Real control is when you're not even in the room, but your voice is still inside their fucking head.**

That's the **Echo Effect.** It's when you condition someone so well that **they hear your words even when you're not around.** Every decision they make, every doubt they have, every risk they consider—**you're there, in their mind, guiding them without lifting a damn finger.**

You don't need to chase people. **You need to become the thought they can't escape.**

How to Get Inside Their Head and Stay There

- **Repeat key phrases until they internalize them.** You ever notice how people start repeating shit without realizing it? **That's because repetition burns ideas into the brain.** Say something often enough—especially when they're emotional, uncertain, or vulnerable—and **it sticks.**

- **Make your words their safety net.** People don't like thinking for themselves. **They want an easy answer, a guiding voice that makes decisions for them.** Make your voice that default. "When in doubt, just remember this…" "You know what I always say…" **Give them mental shortcuts, and they'll start relying on them.**

- **Attach your voice to their emotions.** If you've ever heard an old song and instantly felt something, **you know exactly how this works.** Make sure your words hit them **when they're deep in emotion—excited, scared, angry, relieved.** The stronger the emotional state, **the stronger the imprint.**

- **Leave open loops so they come back for closure.** People hate unfinished thoughts. **Give them something to chew on but don't resolve it.** "I'll tell you what I think later." "You'll see what I mean soon enough." **They'll keep replaying the conversation, waiting for answers that only you can give.**

How to Make Sure the Echo Stays Permanent

- **Get them repeating you to others.** The second they start spreading your message, **it locks in.** Their brain goes, **"I wouldn't be saying this if it weren't true."** Now, **they're reinforcing your words on their own.**

- **Use rhetorical questions that trigger doubt.** "Are you sure that's a good move?" "I mean, do you really trust them?" You don't need to tell them what to think. **Just plant the fucking seed.** They'll do the rest of the work on their own.

- **Tie your voice to their identity.** If they start hearing you as part of who they are—**as their guide, their inner voice, their standard for decision-making—you own them.** Their thoughts will pass through your filter before they even act.

- **Keep reinforcing it over time.** A good manipulator doesn't let the imprint fade. **Drop reminders. Call back to old lessons. Make sure they keep hearing you, even if it's in their own head.**

Bottom Line: If They Hear You When You're Not Around, You've Already Won

The strongest control isn't about force—it's about **becoming part of how they process the fucking world.** If every decision they make feels like **you're there, watching, guiding, commenting in the back of their mind,** you don't need to micromanage them. **They'll police themselves.**

Tactic 10.2 – How to Make People Choose What You Want Before They Realize It

Most people think they make choices. **They don't.** By the time they "decide" on something, **the path has already been laid out for them.** Their brain is just catching up, rationalizing a choice that was never really theirs to begin with.

This is where real control happens. **Not forcing, not convincing—just structuring the options so they naturally pick the one you wanted all along.** By the time they think they're deciding, **they're just walking through a door you built for them.**

And the best part? **They'll believe it was their idea the whole fucking time.**

How to Set Up Decisions So They Choose What You Want

- ◉ **Give them two choices, but make one impossible.** People need to feel like they have options, but **you don't give them real choices—you give them the illusion of choice.** One path is easy, rewarding, and aligned with what you want. **The other is uncomfortable, uncertain, or outright stupid.** They'll pick the "right" one every time **—and they'll think it was entirely up to them.**

- ◉ **Make the decision feel obvious.** People don't like thinking. **They go with whatever feels natural, easy,**

or expected. If you want someone to choose something, **talk about it like it's already a given.** "So when you do this…" "Once you get started on this…" **If they don't stop you to question it, they've already accepted it.**

- **Frame the alternative as a mistake.** You don't need to tell them outright that the other option sucks. **Just plant the idea that it's a bad move.** "Yeah, I mean, some people try that, but it usually doesn't work out." "I knew a guy who did that once… he regretted it." **Now the alternative feels risky, and they'll avoid it without you having to say a damn thing.**

- **Push them toward the decision before they realize it's happening.** Get them nodding, agreeing with small things leading up to the choice. **Make them commit to little steps first.** "Yeah, you're the kind of person who always makes smart moves." "I can already tell you're gonna do the right thing." **They won't want to backpedal on their own words, so they'll follow through.**

How to Make Sure They Never Question Their Decision

- **Make them justify it to themselves.** Once they choose your path, **get them talking about why it was the right move.** The more they explain it, the more they believe it. **By the time they're done rationalizing, they'll defend the decision like it was theirs all along.**

- **Praise their "independence."** People want to feel in control. **Stroke their ego for "making the right call."** "I like that you think for yourself." "That's what I respect about you, you don't let people influence you." **They'll double down on their choice just to keep that self-image intact.**

- ◉ **Make reversing the decision feel like failure.** People hate going back on something once they've committed. **Make the idea of changing their mind feel like weakness.** "I'd be surprised if you backed out now." "I mean, once you've seen the truth, you can't really unsee it." **Now, if they rethink their choice, they're admitting they were wrong—so they won't.**

- ◉ **Attach the decision to their identity.** "You're the kind of person who takes action." "You've always been smart about these things." **Now the choice isn't just about the action—it's about who they are.** Once they accept that, **they'll fight to stay consistent with it.**

Bottom Line: If You Structure the Choice Right, They'll Pick It Every Time

You don't have to force people to choose what you want. **You just have to set it up so it feels like the only real option.** Give them an easy path and a bad one. **Talk about your option like it's already happening.** Make backing out feel like a mistake.

By the time they think they've "made up their mind," **they were never in control to begin with.**

Tactic 10.3: The Ghost Tactic – How to Maintain Control Without Direct Contact

Control isn't about standing over someone and barking orders. **That's weak, obvious, and exhausting.** Real control is when you're not even there, **but they're still acting like you are.** They check themselves before making a move. **They hesitate, wondering what you'd think.** They adjust their behavior, even when you haven't said a goddamn word.

That's the **Ghost Tactic.** It's when your influence lingers, **burned into their head so deep that they start controlling**

themselves. You don't need to chase them down. **They carry your presence with them like a fucking shadow.**

If you do this right, **you don't have to enforce your rules— they will.**

How to Make Sure They Always Feel Your Presence

- **Make them dependent on your approval.** First, you create the habit: **they seek validation, you provide it.** Then, you pull it back. **Make them wonder if they're doing the right thing, make them crave reassurance.** Over time, they'll start anticipating your reaction **before they even act.** That's when you've won.

- **Create "rules" they don't realize they're following.** People get trained into behavior patterns without noticing. **Tie their choices to your expectations.** "You've always been smart about these things." "I know you wouldn't make that mistake." They start making decisions based on **what you'd want—without even realizing it.**

- **Leave them second-guessing.** The best control is when **they're the ones doubting themselves.** If they start wondering what you'd think, **if they hesitate before making a move, if they feel uncomfortable acting without your input—you're locked in.**

- **Make them feel watched, even when they're alone.** A well-placed comment can make them paranoid as fuck. **"I hear things." "I always find out."** It's not about having eyes on them 24/7—it's about making them think you do.

How to Maintain Control Without Constant Contact

- **Reinforce their need for guidance.** Every time they come to you with a decision, **make sure they leave thinking they'd be lost without your input.** "See? You almost made a mistake, good thing we talked." Over time, **they'll stop trusting their own instincts altogether.**

⦿ **Use absence as a weapon.** When someone is too comfortable, **disappear.** Pull back. Make them wonder what happened. **That space makes them crave your presence, reset their behavior, and come back even more eager to please.**

⦿ **Make them repeat your words when you're not there.** "You know what I always say." "I bet you can already guess what I'd think." **Get them saying your phrases, following your rules, thinking in your patterns.** The moment they start echoing you in their head, **you've fucking won.**

⦿ **Create triggers that bring you to mind.** A certain phrase, a specific look, a particular setting—**program their brain to associate those things with you.** That way, even if you're miles away, **the right trigger will make them feel like you're standing right next to them.**

Bottom Line: If They Think About You Before They Act, You Own Them

You don't need to hover over them like a desperate asshole. **You need to make sure they feel your presence even in your silence.** If they hesitate, if they replay your words in their head, if they change their behavior based on what they think you'd want—**congratulations, motherfucker. You don't need to be there to control them anymore.**

They carry your influence with them, everywhere they fucking go. Control that requires presence isn't control. The real power move is silence — when your absence still dictates their behavior. When you're gone and they still obey, you've become their religion.

> *The highest level of control isn't physical —it's psychological residue. When your voice becomes their conscience and your silence feels like judgment, you've gone from influence to infection. You don't live in their head rent-free—you own the deed. By the time they realize it, they'll defend your control like it's their own free will.*

Lesson 11: Setting Traps That Manipulate Minds for You

Tactic 11.1:
Environmental Triggers – How to Control Emotions Through Surroundings

People think they make decisions based on logic. **That's fucking hilarious.** The truth is, **their environment controls them more than their own goddamn mind.** The space they're in, the lighting, the colors, the sounds, the smells—**all of it shapes how they think, feel, and act, whether they realize it or not.**

If you control the environment, **you control the person.** You can make them relaxed or on edge, confident or insecure, dominant or submissive—**without saying a fucking word.** You don't have to argue, convince, or demand. **You just set the scene and let their brain do the rest.**

And the best part? **They'll think it was all their own doing.**

How to Set Up an Environment That Controls People Without Them Knowing

- **Control the space, and you control the mood.** Ever notice how luxury stores are quiet and uncluttered? How interrogation rooms are stark and uncomfortable? **That's not an accident.** People respond to their surroundings without thinking. **If the environment makes them feel a certain way, their behavior follows automatically.**

- **Use lighting and color to trigger emotions.** Bright lights make people alert. **Dim, warm lighting makes them relax.** Red makes people anxious and aggressive. **Blue calms them down.** You want them open and comfortable? **Soft lighting, warm tones, deep chairs.** You want them insecure and on edge? **Bright lights, cold colors, an uncomfortable seat that makes them fidget.**

- **Control the background noise.** Loud environments make people distracted and reactive. **Silence makes them self-conscious.** Play soft music, and they'll feel relaxed. **Use an unpredictable, low-level hum of sound, and they'll feel unsettled without knowing why.**

- **Make them feel small or powerful with space control.** Wide, open spaces make people feel confident and in control. **Small, enclosed spaces make them feel trapped.** If you want someone submissive? **Put them in a chair lower than yours, give them no room to spread out, and make sure the space subtly reminds them they're not in control.**

- **Use physical comfort (or discomfort) to manipulate focus.** A person sitting in a comfortable, warm room with soft chairs and controlled lighting? **They'll let their guard down.** A person in a hard chair, in a slightly too-cold or too-hot room, with flickering lights? **They'll be too distracted to think straight.**

How to Weaponize Environments for Long-Term Control

- **Anchor emotions to specific places.** If you want someone to feel insecure, **make sure every hard conversation happens in the same chair, the same spot, the same setting.** Their brain will start associating the place with feeling off-balance. **Now, they'll start feeling that way the second they sit down—before you even open your mouth.**

- **Set traps that trigger old emotions.** You ever smell something and instantly remember an old memory? **That's anchoring.** Tie a specific song, scent, or object to an emotional state. **Once it's locked in, you can trigger that feeling whenever you need to.**

- **Make your presence linger, even when you're not there.** If someone associates a space with you, **they'll feel your influence even when you're gone.** Your home, your office, the car they ride in with you—**fill it with cues that remind them of you.** Over time, **the environment itself starts controlling their thoughts.**

- **Use unpredictability to fuck with their sense of security.** People feel safe in routine. **Break that, and you break them.** If they walk into a room and never know if it'll be welcoming or cold, bright or dark, comfortable or tense—**they'll be on edge before you even do anything.**

Bottom Line: If You Control the Environment, You Control the Person

People don't think independently. **They react to their surroundings.** If you set the stage right, you don't have to convince them of shit. **They'll feel what you want them to feel, they'll act how you want them to act, and they'll never realize you're the one pulling the strings.**

And if they do realize it? **Too late, motherfucker. The room already got to them.**

Tactic 11.2:
Sensory Manipulation – Use Sounds, Smells & Visuals to Shape Behavior

People are arrogant as fuck. They think their choices come from logic, intelligence, and free will. **Bullshit.** Their brains are getting hijacked 24/7 by things they don't even notice—**sounds, smells, colors, tiny details in their environment that change how they think, feel, and act.**

This isn't persuasion. **This is hacking the subconscious.** If you can control what people see, hear, and smell, **you can control their emotions, their focus, their energy levels, and their fucking decisions—all without saying a word.**

They won't know why they feel different. They won't question why they're suddenly anxious, comfortable, or compliant. **They'll just react.**

And if you've done your job right? **They'll follow exactly the path you laid out for them—without ever realizing they were manipulated.**

How to Use Sensory Triggers to Control the Mind

- **Sound dictates focus and emotion.** Slow, low-pitched sounds make people cautious and alert. **Fast-paced sounds make them anxious.** Soft, rhythmic sounds make them relax. **Want someone calm? Keep the background steady, predictable. Want them uncomfortable? Use uneven noise—sounds that come and go at random, just enough to keep them uneasy.**

- **Silence is a weapon.** People are fucking terrified of silence. **It forces them inward, makes them overanalyze, makes** them self-conscious. If you want someone to crack, **say nothing. Let the silence build.** They'll scramble to fill the void—and that's when they'll slip up.

- **Smell is the fastest way to hijack the brain.** The olfactory system is directly wired to memory and emotion. **One whiff of a familiar scent, and they'll feel something before they even know why.** Tie a specific smell to comfort, stress, safety, or tension. **Once it's anchored, you can trigger that state whenever you want.**

- **Visuals control perception without resistance.** Colors, lighting, spatial design—**they tell the brain how to feel before logic catches up.** Blue is calm. Red is aggressive. Yellow makes people restless. **If you want to make someone feel powerless, surround them with vast, open space and towering structures.** If you want them confident, **enclose the space, give them something sturdy to lean on.**

- **Use contrast to create psychological shifts.** Brightness vs. darkness, loud vs. quiet, open vs. enclosed—**sudden shifts fuck with the brain and make people hyper-aware.** Keep everything stable, and they'll relax. **Throw in a sudden change, and they'll feel vulnerable as fuck.**

How to Weaponize Sensory Manipulation for Total Control

- **Make them associate comfort with you.** If they only feel **safe, at ease, and validated in your presence,** they'll crave being around you. **Anchor positive feelings to your space, your scent, your voice.** Once their brain fuses that connection, **they'll chase it without realizing why.**

- **Tie their worst emotions to your enemies.** If there's someone you want them to distance themselves from,

make sure every mention of that person comes with negativity. Talk about them when the room is tense, bring them up in moments of frustration. **Their brain will start making the connection automatically.**

- **Use environmental changes to apply pressure.** Want someone to sweat? **Turn up the heat just a little. Make them physically uncomfortable.** Want them anxious? **Drop the background noise for a second—make the silence hit hard.** Want them compliant? **Lower the lights, soften the sounds, drop their defenses.**

- **Make them dependent on a specific trigger.** If they associate a certain sound, smell, or setting with you, **they'll react to it even when you're gone.** The second they hear the familiar tone of your voice, smell your cologne, or see something that reminds them of your space, **their brain will go right back to the conditioned state.**

Bottom Line: If You Control Their Senses, You Control Their Reality

People don't think about this shit. **They just feel it.** Their brain reacts before their logic catches up. If you learn to **control the sights, sounds, and smells around them, you control their emotions, their decisions, their fucking instincts.**

And if they don't realize they're being manipulated? **Even better. That means it's working.**

Tactic 11.3:
Social Conditioning – How to Make a Group Enforce Your Control for You

People don't think for themselves. **They follow the crowd, crave approval, and fear being the outsider more than they fear being fucking wrong.** You don't have to control every individual—**you just have to control the group.** Once you get the collective working in your favor, **they'll do the dirty work for you.**

This is social conditioning. **It's how cults operate, how dictators stay in power, how weak men get eaten alive while the real players sit back and watch.** You don't need to demand obedience. **You make it so stepping out of line means losing the acceptance, safety, and approval of the group.** And since nobody wants to be on the outside looking in, **they'll police themselves before you ever have to.**

How to Turn a Group into a Control System

- **Make them fear isolation more than they fear you.** The second someone believes that **questioning you means losing their status, their relationships, or their place in the hierarchy,** they won't fight back. **They'll self-correct just to stay inside the group.**

- **Create an "us vs. them" mentality.** If you define an enemy—**an outsider, an opposition, a common threat** —people will cling to the group for safety. The best part? **It doesn't even have to be real.** People just need something to rally against.

- **Set unwritten rules that nobody wants to break.** You don't need to say, "If you question me, you're done." **You make it so questioning you automatically makes someone an outsider.** "Oh, you sound just like them." "Funny how the people who don't get it always say the same shit." **Now, stepping out of line means social suicide.**

- **Make obedience the group's culture.** In a strong social system, **people don't obey because they're scared of you. They obey because they don't want to be the only one not doing it.** Once the majority is on your side, **anyone who resists looks like the crazy one.**

How to Make the Group Defend You Without Being Told

- **Encourage them to call out "disloyalty" before you have to.** If you've set up the system right, **people will start attacking anyone who questions you before you even notice it happening.** They'll argue on your behalf, enforce the rules, and make sure everyone else stays in line. **You don't have to punish anyone—they'll punish each other.**

- **Reward those who enforce the system.** The best way to keep control? **Make people feel important when they defend you.** If they go after someone who challenges your influence, **give them praise. Make them feel like they're protecting something bigger than themselves.** Before long, **they'll be competing to be the most loyal follower.**

- **Plant informants without calling them that.** Make people feel like they have a "special" role. "Hey, keep an eye on things for me." "Let me know if you hear anything weird." **Now you've got built-in surveillance. They'll snitch on each other just to stay in your favor.**

- **Punish silently, reward publicly.** When someone steps out of line, **you don't have to scream at them—you just pull away.** Make them feel distant, ignored, like they fucked up. When they correct themselves? **Welcome them back like nothing happened.** The message is clear: **Follow the system, and you stay in good standing. Step out, and you get shut out.**

If You Control the Group, You Control the Individual

You don't need to micromanage people. **You need to make them fear being an outsider more than they fear following you.** Once the group is enforcing the rules for you, **your influence is permanent.**

And the best part? They won't even realize they're not thinking for themselves. The most dangerous battlefield isn't the mind — it's the world the mind reacts to. Once you own the room, the sound, the air, and the people inside it, you don't need orders or threats. The environment itself becomes your enforcer.

> **The battlefield isn't the mind anymore— it's the atmosphere. When the room obeys you, when the sound bends emotion, when the group enforces your rules without question—you've crossed from manipulation into architecture. You're not steering people. You're engineering gravity. Everything falls your way because it has no other choice.**

Chapter Aftermath

You didn't just win the argument—you *preloaded the outcome*. You shaped the air, the mood, the sounds, the fucking chair they sat in. You made their emotions automatic, their decisions predictable, and their resistance non-existent. That's not influence. That's *engineering*. The best control doesn't happen when people obey you—it happens when they obey *themselves*, because you taught their instincts how to kneel.

By the time they react, they won't even know why. They'll just feel something and move exactly how you wanted—like it was always their idea. Their comfort? Yours. Their fear? Yours. Their memory of who they are? Rewritten by a smell, a phrase, a flick of lighting you set weeks ago. That's the power of subliminal warfare—**they never see the strings, because you taught them to love the cage.**

CHAPTER FIVE

<u>The Science of Confidence</u>

Confidence isn't some fluffy "believe in yourself" bullshit. It's a weapon. And in this chapter, I'll show you how to sharpen it until it cuts through any room like a hot knife through a pile of insecure motherfuckers. This isn't about fake smiles or cheesy motivational crap—it's about turning yourself into a walking, talking force of nature that people can't ignore even if they wanted to.

*We start with **The Science of Confidence**, where you'll learn how to walk, talk, and move like you own the goddamn planet. It's not just about presence—it's about overpowering weak-minded people without even opening your mouth. Add in the **"No Hesitation" Rule**, and you'll understand why certainty is the ultimate flex. Hesitation smells like fear, and fear makes you prey. We don't do prey.*

*Finally, we'll wrap it up with **The Psychology of Making People Want to Follow You**. This is where real power lives—not in chasing people, but in making them chase you. Controlled indifference and scarcity are the hooks that keep them addicted. You'll learn how to make people emotionally invest in you* *without giving them shit in return. Throw in a little mystery, and they'll be obsessed without even knowing why. By the end of this chapter, you won't just walk into a room—you'll own it. And everyone else? They'll either follow you, fear you, or get the fuck out of your way.*

Lesson 12: The Science of Confidence–
How to Manufacture Presence

Tactic 12.1:

How to Walk, Talk, and Overpower Without Saying a Damn Word

Confidence isn't just an attitude—it's a goddamn weapon. It's the loaded gun you carry without ever having to pull the trigger because just the sight of it makes people back the fuck off. Most people think confidence is about *feeling* good about yourself. Bullshit. Confidence is about making other people *feel* small in your presence. It's psychological dominance. When you walk into a room, people should feel it before they even see you. Your presence alone should send a message: *I own this fucking space, and you're just visiting.* You're not there to blend in, play nice, or seek approval. You're there to **control the goddamn environment** without saying a single word.

Most people shuffle in like timid little rats, hoping not to be noticed—nervous energy leaking out of every twitch, glance, and awkward smile. Not you. You're going to **command** attention, not ask for it. You'll own the room the moment you step inside, and you'll do it without needing to impress a single soul. Why? Because real power isn't about proving anything. It's about walking in like you've got nothing to prove—and making everyone else feel like they do.

1. Walk Like You've Already Won

Your stride should be **deliberate, unhurried, and controlled**— like you know exactly where you're going and why. People who rush look desperate. People who hesitate look lost. **You? You move like the world bends to your will.**

- Keep your shoulders back. Slumped posture screams weakness.

- Walk with steady, even steps—no fidgeting, no hesitation.

- Never look at the ground. Keep your eyes straight ahead like you own the fucking planet.

2. The Power of Standing Still

Most insecure assholes are constantly shifting, adjusting, or making nervous movements. That's prey behavior. **Predators move with intention.**

- When you stop moving, **stop completely**. Stand like a statue. **Stillness is power.**

- Keep your feet planted like you belong wherever the fuck you are.

- When you talk, move *slowly*—every motion should feel calculated, not frantic.

3. Speak Like You Expect to Be Heard

Losers raise their voices or talk too fast because they're desperate for validation. The truly powerful? They don't chase attention—it comes to them.

- **Lower your voice.** People lean in for deep, steady tones. Nervous little yaps get ignored.

- **Pause before answering.** It makes people *wait* on you, and that's power.

- **Minimal words, maximum impact.** Don't ramble—state your point and let the silence do the heavy lifting.

4. Make People Feel Small Without Saying a Word

When you own your presence, weak people instinctively shrink around you. Here's how you accelerate that:

- **Hold eye contact longer than is comfortable.** Most people look away first—it's an automatic sign of submission.

- **Don't overreact to anything.** The more neutral your facial expressions, the more dominant you seem.

- **Take up space.** Lean back, stretch out—make it clear you aren't adjusting for anyone.

The way you walk, stand, and talk tells people everything they need to know about whether they should respect you or dismiss you. **Confidence isn't a thought, it's a presence. You don't demand attention—you fucking command it.**

Tactic 12.2:
The "No Hesitation" Rule—Why Certainty Creates Power

Hesitation is the silent alarm that tells the world you're unsure, insecure, and easy to dominate. It's the crack in the armor that lets doubt seep in—not just into *you*, but into everyone watching you. When you pause to question yourself, second-guess your moves, or overthink your next words, you're not being "careful." You're broadcasting weakness like a flashing neon sign: *"I'm not sure of myself, feel free to challenge me."* And guess what? The world fucking will.

Confidence isn't about being right all the time. It's about **acting like you are**, even when you're winging it. The **"No Hesitation" Rule** is simple: whatever you do, do it with absolute conviction. You make decisions quickly. You speak without second-guessing. You move like every step was pre-planned by a goddamn mastermind—even if you're making it up as you go. **Hesitation invites doubt. Certainty commands respect.** People don't follow the smartest person in the room; they follow the one who *acts* like they know exactly what the fuck they're doing.

1. The Psychology Behind Certainty

People are hardwired to respond to confidence. Why? Because most of them are weak, insecure little sheep looking for someone to tell them what to do. When you hesitate, it triggers their instincts: *"Maybe this guy doesn't know what he's doing."* But when you speak with conviction—when you say something like it's gospel—they won't question it. They'll believe it because you believe it.

- **Fact:** The actual content of your words matters less than how you deliver them.

- **Reality:** People don't follow facts; they follow *certainty*.

- **Truth:** Fake confidence beats real insecurity every damn time.

2. Speak First, Think Later (Yes, You Heard That Right)

Overthinking kills momentum. Instead of analyzing every possible outcome like some spineless corporate douchebag stuck in a board meeting, just fucking say it. Make your point. Plant your flag. Even if you're wrong, you'll own it so hard people will doubt *themselves* before they doubt you.

- **Pro tip:** If you realize mid-sentence that you're wrong—**double down**. Say it louder, with more conviction.

- ◉ **Bonus move:** If someone challenges you, hit them with, *"That's exactly what I said, you just weren't smart enough to get it."* Instant psychological dominance.

3. Decisions: Snap, Don't Stall

Indecision is the kiss of death. Leaders make decisions fast because speed = control. Waiting around, weighing every little option? That's what losers do while the real players are already ten steps ahead.

- ◉ **Rule:** If it takes longer than 10 seconds to decide, you're overthinking. Pick an option and move.

- ◉ **Tactic:** Frame every choice as if both outcomes benefit you. That way, whatever you pick feels like the right move—because it is.

4. The Art of Owning Your Mistakes (Without Looking Weak)

Now, let's get real—sometimes you'll fuck up. But here's the trick: **never apologize for acting with certainty.** If you're wrong, pivot. Reframe. Say it was part of a bigger plan. People respect consistency more than perfection.

- ◉ **Wrong?** Say, *"That was a calculated risk. I knew the odds, and I'd make the same call again."*

- ◉ **Criticized?** Respond with, *"Good thing I don't take advice from people who've never done shit."*

Hesitation is for the weak. Certainty is a weapon. You don't have to be right—you just have to sound like you are. **Move fast. Speak boldly. Act like every decision you make is carved in stone.** And if you screw up? **Own it like you meant to do it.** That's how you win. Every. Damn. Time.

Tactic 12.3:
The Dominance Effect: Make Yourself Big, Make Them Feel Tiny

Power isn't just about what you say—it's about how you **exist** in a room. The way you stand, the space you take up, the energy you project—it all sends a message: *"I'm in control, and you're not."* This is the **Dominance Effect**. It's not some soft-ass self-help mantra about "positive vibes" or "owning your space." Fuck that. This is about psychological warfare—**making yourself impossible to ignore while shrinking everyone else into irrelevant background noise.**

Most people walk into a room trying to fit in. That's loser behavior. You're not here to blend in; you're here to **dominate**. To be the gravitational force that pulls attention without asking for it. This isn't about arrogance. It's about **deliberate, calculated presence**—turning your body language into a weapon that makes people feel small, insecure, and off-balance without you having to lift a finger.

1. The Power Stance: Own the Space You Stand On

First rule of physical dominance: **take up space like you fucking paid for it.** Most people shrink themselves because they're afraid of being noticed. Not you.

- ◉ **Feet shoulder-width apart.** No timid, pigeon-toed bullshit. Plant yourself like the ground owes you rent.

- ◉ **Shoulders back, chest slightly out.** This isn't about puffing up like some insecure gym bro—it's about projecting quiet, unshakable authority.

- ◉ **Hands visible, relaxed, but controlled.** Clenched fists scream insecurity. Loose, confident hands say, *"I've got nothing to prove because I've already won."*

•**Bonus move:** When sitting, don't cross your arms like a defensive little bitch. Sit wide, lean back, and own the space like it's yours—because it is.

2. The Art of Making People Feel Small (Without Saying Shit)

You don't need to insult anyone to make them feel insignificant. **Your presence alone can do the job.**

- ◉ **Stand slightly closer than "comfortable."** Not enough to be creepy—just enough to subtly invade their space. Watch them step back. That's submission without a word.

- ◉ **Look down your nose, even if they're taller.** It's a subtle tilt of the chin that screams, *"You're beneath me."*

- ◉ **Slow, deliberate movements.** Fast, jerky motions = nervous energy. Slow, controlled movements = *"I move when I fucking feel like it."*

3. Command the Room Without Chasing Attention

Here's the mindfuck: the less you *try* to get attention, the more you'll get it. People are drawn to those who act like they don't need an audience.

- ◉ **Walk like you have a destination, even if you don't.** Purposeful movement signals importance.

- ◉ **Pause in the doorway.** When you enter a room, stop for half a second—just enough for people to notice. It's a subconscious power play that says, *"I'm here. You're welcome."*

- ◉ **Own the silence.** Don't rush to fill gaps in conversation. Let others squirm while you control the tempo.

4. The Energy Transfer: Make Them Feel Your Presence

Presence isn't just physical—it's energetic. It's the unspoken tension in the room when you walk in. Here's how to crank that shit up:

- **Direct, unbroken eye contact.** Not wide-eyed psycho shit—just calm, steady, and unflinching. Make them look away first. That's a win.

- **Breathe deeply and slowly.** Shallow breathers are anxious. Deep, controlled breathing signals calm dominance.

- **Don't mirror weak body language.** If someone's slouched or fidgeting, resist the urge to mimic. Hold your ground, and watch them unconsciously adjust to you.

The **Dominance Effect** isn't about aggression. It's about **control.** Control of your body, your space, and the psychological environment around you. **You don't need to speak to make people feel small. You just need to exist like you're too big to ignore.** And trust me—they'll feel it. Every. Damn. Time.

Tactic 12.4:
Using Strategic Eye Contact to Force Submission

You don't need to raise your voice, throw insults, or puff out your chest to make someone feel insignificant. **Real power isn't loud— it's silent, sharp, and suffocating.** The most savage form of dominance is psychological. It's about walking into a room and making people feel like they're standing in the shadow of a fucking mountain. No threats. No words. Just pure, unfiltered presence that crushes their self-esteem like a bug under your boot.

This isn't about being a bully. It's about control. **Making people feel small isn't petty—it's tactical.** It keeps you in the driver's seat without wasting energy. When you can dismantle someone's confidence without opening your mouth, that's when you know you've mastered psychological warfare.

1. Mastering the Art of Disinterest

Nothing stings more than being ignored. Want to shrink someone's ego? Treat them like background noise.

- **The "Glance and Dismiss" Move:** Look at them briefly —just long enough to register their existence—then look away like they're not worth your attention. No acknowledgment. No reaction. Just indifference. It hits harder than any insult.

- **Dead Eyes:** When they're talking, keep your face neutral, your eyes flat, and your expression blank. No nodding, no smiling, no engagement. It makes them feel like their words are floating in the void.

- **Bonus move:** If they ask a question, pause like you're deciding if it's even worth answering. That hesitation? It's a dagger straight to the ego.

2. Owning Space Like You're Entitled to It

People instinctively shrink around those who take up space unapologetically. **Your body language should scream, "I belong here. You don't."**

- **The Wide Stance:** Stand with your feet shoulder-width apart, arms relaxed but slightly away from your body. You're claiming space without asking permission.

- **Lean Back, Never Forward:** Leaning forward shows interest. Leaning back says, *"Impress me… if you can."*

- **Slow, Deliberate Movements:** Fast, jittery motions are for anxious, insecure people. Move like you've got all the time in the world—because you do. Their need for validation is the only thing on a deadline.

3. The Power of Deliberate Pauses

Silence can be deafening when used right. It creates tension, forces people to fill the gap, and makes them feel uncomfortable without knowing why.

- **Hold Eye Contact... Then Pause:** Lock eyes for a second longer than is socially comfortable, then break it slowly—like you've already sized them up and dismissed them.

- **Let Questions Hang:** When someone asks you something, wait. Let the silence stretch. They'll either start over-explaining or stumble, trying to fill the awkward gap. Either way, you've got them.

- **Micro Pauses Mid-Sentence:** When speaking, pause just before delivering your key point. It makes people lean in, desperate for the conclusion—subconsciously putting you in control.

4. The Cold Read Tactic

This is where you really fuck with someone's head. **Act like you can see through them.**

- **Quick Scans:** Look them up and down once—subtly, but noticeably—then smirk slightly like you've already judged them and found them lacking.

- **Neutral Compliments:** Say things like, *"Interesting choice,"* without clarifying if it's good or bad. The ambiguity makes them spiral internally, wondering what you meant.

- **"I Know" Statements:** Drop vague comments like, *"Yeah, I can tell,"* after they say something. It makes them paranoid, thinking you've figured something out about them they didn't reveal.

You don't need to be the loudest, the strongest, or the smartest person in the room to dominate it. **You just need to master the**

art of psychological pressure. Make them question themselves. Make them uncomfortable. **Make them feel small without ever saying a fucking word.** That's real power. That's control. And the best part? **They'll have no idea why they feel that way—only that they do.**

Confidence isn't a feeling — it's a performance. The weak wait to feel powerful. The strong act powerful until everyone else starts believing it for them. You don't build confidence — you broadcast it until the world tunes in.

> *Confidence isn't about believing in yourself—it's about making everyone else believe in you before you even open your mouth. You don't think powerful. You act powerful until the world adjusts to your script. Every movement, every pause, every stare is a command disguised as body language. You're not blending in— you're bending reality. Own the space or get swallowed by it.*

Lesson 13: Tactical Assertiveness–How to Speak With Authority

Tactic 13.1:
Commanding Respect with Silence and Sound

Respect isn't given. It's not earned with polite handshakes, fake smiles, or by being the "nice guy" everyone likes. **Fuck that.** Respect is **taken**—ripped from the minds of people who didn't even realize they were about to hand it over. You don't need to be the loudest motherfucker in the room to get it. In fact, the loudest guy? He's usually the weakest—screaming because he knows no one's really listening.

The secret? **Mastering your voice and your silence.** That's right—**silence** is just as powerful as sound. When you control both, you control people. You make them lean in when you talk, shut the fuck up when you pause, and squirm when you don't say a damn thing. This isn't about shouting people down. It's about creating a presence so sharp, so undeniable, that even a whisper feels like a goddamn roar.

1. The Power of Volume Control (Louder Isn't Stronger, Dumbass)

Weak people yell to cover their insecurities. Strong people? They **lower** their voice, forcing others to lean in. You don't beg for attention—you **make** them give it to you.

- ⊙ **Lower your voice slightly.** It forces people to focus, making every word feel deliberate, like it's carved in stone.

- ⊙ **Never shout unless you intend to destroy.** If you do raise your voice, do it once, with purpose. Make it feel like an earthquake—rare, but impossible to ignore.

- ⊙ **Bonus move:** When everyone's loud, go quiet. It's psychological judo—your silence becomes the loudest thing in the room.

2. Mastering the Art of the Pause (Weaponized Silence)

Most people talk like they're afraid of dead air. They fill every second with pointless noise, thinking it makes them sound confident. **It doesn't. It makes them sound desperate.**

- ⊙ **Pause before you speak.** Just a second or two. It makes people think, *"What's he about to say?"* You've already got their attention before a word leaves your mouth.

- **Strategic mid-sentence pauses.** When you're about to drop a key point, pause. Let the tension build. People lean in, hungry for the punchline you're holding hostage.

- **Own the silence after you speak.** Don't rush to fill the gap. Let your words hang in the air like smoke after a gunshot.

3. Tone: The Hidden Blade in Your Voice

Your tone is the difference between sounding like a leader or sounding like some insecure dipshit trying too hard.

- **Controlled, steady tone.** No wobbles, no upticks at the end of sentences. You're not *asking*—you're stating facts.

- **Drop your tone slightly when making a point.** It signals finality, like, *"This isn't up for debate."*

- **Inflect with purpose.** Want to sound sarcastic? Flatten your tone. Want to sound deadly serious? Lower it, slow it down, and stare straight through the person you're talking to.

4. Cutting People Off (Without Looking Like an Asshole... Even Though You Are)

Sometimes, people don't know when to shut the fuck up. That's where you come in.

- **The Interrupt-and-Pause Technique:** Cut in with a simple, "Hold on," then pause. The silence makes it clear you're taking control.

- **Overlap Strategy:** Start talking over them slowly, not aggressively. Your calmness makes their noise feel chaotic.

- **Eye Contact Domination:** If someone keeps talking, don't argue—just stare at them, deadpan. Eventually, they'll feel the weight of your silence and stop.

Bottom Line

Respect isn't asked for. It's commanded. Your voice is a weapon, and silence is the blade you sharpen it with. **Speak less, say more. Lower your voice, raise their attention. Pause, and watch them crumble in the gap.** You don't need to shout to dominate. **You just need to sound like you don't give a fuck if they're listening—because that's exactly when they'll listen the most.**

Tactic 13.2:
How to Subtly Cut Off People Who Talk Too Much

Let's be real—**some people just don't know when to shut the fuck up.** They ramble on, vomiting words like it's going to earn them respect. But here's the thing: **the more they talk, the weaker they look.** And if you let them keep going, you look weak too—like you're too afraid to step in and take control. That's not how we roll.

Cutting people off isn't just about silencing them—it's about **reclaiming dominance** in the conversation without looking like a raging asshole (even though, let's face it, you probably are). The trick is to do it with **precision, confidence, and zero hesitation**. When you do it right, they don't even realize you've just verbally bitch-slapped them. They just stop talking, and suddenly, **you're the one in control.**

1. The Power Interrupt: Short, Sharp, and Brutal

When someone's rambling, you don't need to match their energy. You need to **break** it.

- **The One-Word Kill Shot:** Drop a firm, *"Enough,"* *"Stop,"* or *"Hold up."* No emotion, no explanation—just pure authority. It's like slamming a door in their face mid-sentence.

- **Bonus move:** Combine it with a slight hand gesture—palm out, like you're physically stopping their words. It's simple, effective, and makes them feel like a toddler being told to sit the fuck down.

2. The Overlap Strategy: Talk Right Over Them (But Smooth as Hell)

Sometimes you don't need to wait for a pause—**you create one.**

- **Start Talking Mid-Sentence:** Don't raise your voice to overpower them. Just start speaking in a calm, controlled tone. It forces them to either shut up or look like an idiot trying to talk over you.

- **The Calm Crusher:** While they're still yapping, lean slightly forward, make eye contact, and start your sentence with, *"Here's the thing…"* or *"What actually matters is…"* They'll stop out of sheer confusion, and boom—you've hijacked the conversation.

3. The Dead-Eye Silence: Psychological Warfare 101

If you want to be a real savage, don't say anything at all. **Just stare.**

- **Blank Expression, Hard Stare:** No nodding, no smiling —just a cold, bored look like their words are background noise. Eventually, their brain short-circuits, and they'll trail off into awkward silence.

- **The "Look Away" Move:** Mid-sentence, look away like you've completely lost interest. Check your watch, glance at your phone, or even yawn. It's disrespectful in the most subtle, soul-crushing way possible.

4. The Redirect Technique: Take Control Without a Fight

If you want to be slick about it, **redirect** the conversation so it looks like you're just "moving things along."

- **Cut with Purpose:** Interrupt with, *"Let's get back to the point,"* or *"We're getting off track—here's what matters."* It frames you as the leader, not the jerk.

- **Ask a Direct Question:** Jump in with a sharp question that shifts focus. *"Okay, but what's the takeaway here?"* This forces them to stop rambling and puts you back in control.

5. The Humiliation Hook (For When You Want to Leave a Mark)

If someone really deserves it—like the office blowhard who thinks they're the smartest person in the room—**go for the jugular.**

- **Sarcastic Sniper Shot:** *"Wow, you really like the sound of your own voice, huh?"*

- **Brutal Efficiency:** *"Are you almost done, or should I grab a chair?"*

- **Cold Precision:** *"Is there a point to this, or are we just doing word aerobics now?"*

This isn't for every situation, but when the gloves come off, these lines hit harder than a slap to the face—and they'll think twice before running their mouth around you again.

Cutting people off isn't rude—it's strategic. You're not here to be polite. You're here to **own the fucking conversation.**

Whether it's with a sharp word, a cold stare, or a brutal punchline, the goal is the same: **shut them down, take control, and make it look effortless.** Because in the game of psychological warfare, the person who controls the talking controls the power. **And that person is you.**

Tactic 13.3:
Indifference & Scarcity: The Art of Making People Chase

You want to know the real secret to power? **Stop giving a fuck.** That's right—**controlled indifference** is the ultimate psychological weapon. Nothing makes people obsess over you more than acting like you don't give a shit whether they exist or not. Combine that with a little bit of **scarcity**—making yourself hard to get—and suddenly, you've got people crawling over broken glass just to get your attention.

Humans are wired for this kind of mindfuck. **We crave what we can't have and ignore what's easily available.** That's why desperate people never get what they want—they're too busy begging for it. But when you flip the script, when you act like *you're* the prize, people start chasing *you*. It's not magic. It's psychology. And if you do it right, you can make anyone addicted to your attention—or more accurately, your lack of it.

1. The Power of Indifference: Stop Caring, Start Winning

The less you care, the more they do. **Indifference isn't passive —it's strategic.** You're not being cold because you're emotionless; you're being cold because it makes people burn for your approval.

- ⦿ **Rule #1:** Never react emotionally. Whether it's praise, criticism, or drama—*stay cool.* Your indifference makes people desperate to get a reaction out of you.

- **Act Like You Have Options.** Even if you don't. The vibe should always be, *"I could take it or leave it."* That's the energy that drives people fucking crazy.

- **Bonus Move:** When someone's trying hard to impress you, respond with, *"Oh, that's cool."* No enthusiasm. No over-the-top reaction. Just flat, casual disinterest. Watch how fast they try harder.

2. Scarcity: Why Being Less Available = More Valuable

People don't value what's always there. **Scarcity creates demand.** When you're hard to reach, hard to read, and hard to get—suddenly, everyone wants a piece.

- **The Rule of Absence:** Don't always be available. Make people wait. Make them wonder where you are, what you're doing, and why you're not answering.

- **Disappear Strategically:** Pull back when people expect you to show up. Skip events. Go quiet for a while. When you reappear, it feels like an *event*—and people treat you like one.

- **Bonus Move:** End conversations first. Always. Leave them wanting more. Even if it's going great, cut it short. *"Alright, I've got to run. Catch you later."* Boom. Now they're hooked.

3. The Push-Pull Effect: Emotional Whiplash for Maximum Control

Want to make someone addicted to your attention? **Mix indifference with occasional validation.** Give them a taste of approval, then pull it back.

- ⦿ **Push:** Act distant, disengaged, hard to read.

- ⦿ **Pull:** Drop a compliment out of nowhere. *"You know, you're actually pretty sharp."* Then go back to being distant.

- ⦿ **Result:** They get emotional whiplash, constantly chasing that next "pull" moment. It's like emotional gambling—they never know when the next win is coming, so they keep playing.

4. Control the Frame: You're the Prize, Not Them

Most people approach relationships—whether personal or professional—with the wrong mindset. **They think they need to prove themselves.** Fuck that. The mindset is simple: *"I'm the prize. You're lucky to be in my presence."*

- ⦿ **Don't Over-Explain Yourself.** People who talk too much about their value seem insecure. Let your presence speak for itself.

- ⦿ **Let Them Chase.** If they pull back, don't chase after them. Stay put. Your lack of reaction will pull them right back in.

- ⦿ **Bonus Move:** When someone asks for your opinion, delay your response. Let them feel the weight of your silence. When you finally speak, your words will feel more important—because they had to wait for them.

Power isn't about being liked. It's about being wanted— and not giving a fuck if you are. Indifference makes people crave your attention. Scarcity makes them desperate for your presence. **You don't chase. You attract. You don't explain. You exist.** And when you master this? **People will chase you like you're the last shot of whiskey in a dry county.**

Tactic 13.4
How to Make People Invest in You Emotionally

You want real power? **Get inside their fucking heads.** Not just where they think about you occasionally—I'm talking full-on, rent-free real estate in their mind. **Emotional investment** is the ultimate control tool. When someone's emotionally hooked, you don't have to chase, beg, or convince them of shit. They'll do the work for you. They'll justify, rationalize, and even defend your bullshit because they're too deep in the emotional quicksand to pull themselves out.

But here's the catch: **you don't get people to invest by being nice.** That's amateur hour. You make them invest by creating a cocktail of emotional highs and lows, giving them just enough to crave more, but never enough to feel secure. It's psychological crack—once they get a taste, they'll keep coming back for another hit.

1. The Hook: Start Strong, Pull Back Fast

The first step? **Get their attention.** The second step? **Take it away.**

- **Step 1:** Be engaging, charismatic, even a little intense. Make them feel like they've just met the most interesting person on the planet—you.

- **Step 2: Disappear.** Go cold. Stop responding. Be "busy." This sudden shift creates an emotional gap they'll scramble to fill.

- **Bonus Move:** Right when they start pulling away, reel them back with a simple message: *"Thinking about you."* That's it. Short, vague, and it resets the hook deeper.

2. The Emotional Rollercoaster: Highs Hit Harder After Lows

People don't get addicted to consistency—they get addicted to **contrast.** You've got to create emotional peaks and valleys.

- ◉ **Give them validation:** Compliments, attention, whatever makes them feel good.

- ◉ **Then withdraw:** No explanation. Just distance. Let them sit in the uncertainty.

- ◉ **Result:** Their brain associates the *high* with you, and the *low* makes them crave the next high even more. It's the same psychological trick slot machines use—**random rewards create obsession.**

3. Vulnerability as a Weapon (But Only Yours)

Here's where it gets sneaky. **People bond over vulnerability, but that doesn't mean you have to actually be vulnerable.**

- ◉ **Controlled Vulnerability:** Share something that *seems* personal but isn't really. It makes people feel like they've cracked your shell, creating a false sense of intimacy.

- ◉ **Flip the Script:** Get *them* to open up. Ask questions that dig deep:

  - *"What's the biggest risk you've ever taken?"*

  - *"What's something most people don't know about you?"*

- ◉ **Why it works:** The more *they* share, the more emotionally invested *they* become. People confuse opening up with connection—**even if you don't actually give a shit.**

4. The Scarcity Trigger: Make Them Work for It

People don't value what's easy. If you're always available, you're boring. If you're a little out of reach, you're a challenge—and humans fucking love challenges.

- **Be unpredictable:** Sometimes you respond right away. Sometimes you disappear for days. Keep them guessing.

- **Don't over-commit:** Make them work for your time and attention. The harder they work, the more invested they become.

- **Bonus Move:** Occasionally cancel plans last minute with a casual, *"Something came up."* No explanation. It drives people nuts, and they'll try even harder next time.

5. Leave Breadcrumbs, Not Closure

The key to long-term emotional control? **Never give full closure.**

- **End conversations on your terms.** Even if they're intense, just say, *"I've got to go—talk later."*

- **Be mysterious:** Drop vague comments like, *"There's a lot you don't know about me."* Then refuse to elaborate. Their imagination will do the rest of the work.

- **Ghost-lighting:** A mix of ghosting and breadcrumbing. Go radio silent for a while, then pop back in with a casual, *"Hey, just thought of you."* It keeps them hooked, wondering, *"Why now?"*

Emotional investment isn't about connection—it's about control. You create the highs and lows, you decide when they feel close, and you pull back just enough to keep them chasing. **You don't get hooked—they do.** And once they're in deep, it's game over. **Because when someone's emotionally invested,**

they'll do anything to keep you around—even if you're the one pulling the strings.

> *Authority isn't volume. It's gravity. When you speak, people should feel like they're being pulled toward a black hole that only you control. Every word should land like a verdict. Every silence should hang like a warning. This isn't about earning respect —it's about making it non-negotiable. You don't raise your voice; you raise the room's blood pressure.*

Chapter Aftermath

Confidence isn't some magical trait you hope shows up—it's a system you install like a fucking operating system. You train your body, your voice, your silence, and your presence to scream authority whether you feel it or not. And once the room starts adjusting to *you*? That's when you know you've stopped performing confidence and started *broadcasting power*.

You don't just walk in—they react. You don't ask—you state. You don't beg for respect—you make people *feel* smaller just by existing louder. That's the point of this chapter: not to make you feel better about yourself, but to make everyone else feel like you're ten feet tall and bulletproof. And once they believe that? They'll follow, fold, or fuck off—because there's no room for hesitation when you walk like the world owes you rent.

CHAPTER SIX

The Psychology of Negotiation

Forcing People To Bend To Your Will: Negotiation isn't a polite conversation—it's a goddamn battlefield. **You're not here to "meet in the middle" or "find common ground."** You're here to win, to manipulate, and to walk away with everything while the other side thinks they scored a deal. **Chapter 6 is your war manual.** It's about psychological dominance, where every word, pause, and tactic is designed to break the other person down without them even realizing it. From controlling the first move to framing the entire negotiation, you'll learn how to set traps they can't escape—making them feel like they're in control while you're the one pulling every string.

But this isn't just about quick wins. **It's about long-term control.** You'll master the art of strategic concessions, using fake choices and false urgency to force decisions. You'll learn how to weaponize silence, time, and even failure to make people desperate for your approval. And when it's time to walk away? **You'll do it like a fucking assassin—calm, calculated, and always leaving them wanting more.** This chapter doesn't teach you how to negotiate. It teaches you how to **own the negotiation**—because in the end, it's not about compromise. **It's about conquest**

Lesson 14: Setting the Frame

Tactic 14.1:
Controlling the Opening Gambit: Let Them Go First &
Never Take the First Offer

Negotiation isn't chess. It's an ambush with paperwork. The first one to talk usually hands over their throat, smiling. Every rookie mistake starts with the same disease — the need to sound smart early. The pros? They sit back, shut up, and watch the other side hang themselves with their own words. You let them speak first because every syllable they drop is free intel, and you don't waste free ammo.

The First to Speak Loses the Frame

The second they open their mouth, they give away everything — their range, their desperation, their priorities. You can see it in their tone, their breathing, their goddamn nervous laughter. They think they're being professional; you're reading them like a busted poker hand. Let them anchor the price, define the terms, spill their "bottom line." The first number they say is rarely real — it's bait to test your reaction. Don't bite. Nod once. Say nothing. Let silence stretch until it's awkward. Humans can't stand dead air — they'll start sweetening the deal just to make the silence stop. That's control. That's dominance.

Harvest the Intel While They Bleed Confidence

While they ramble, you're dissecting. You're not taking notes — you're taking inventory: tone, hesitation, ego, insecurity. When they justify something twice, you just found the soft spot. When they rush a sentence, you just found what they're hiding. Write down their buzzwords, because those are levers. The more they explain, the more naked they get. Keep your face neutral, eyes steady. The less you give them, the more they project their own fear into the silence. Every pause you hold costs them confidence.

The Counter-Anchor: Flip the Trap and Own the Math

Now comes the reversal. They think they set the frame — you're about to tear it apart. Use their own number as a mirror, not a wall. "So you're saying you're at $8K because of production costs? That's interesting." That one line flips the power. You acknowledge it, re-frame it, and then re-anchor higher. Calm. Measured. "Here's what makes sense to me — $12K, tied to deliverables, not hours." You didn't argue; you dictated. They'll start defending their number again, which means they're defending *your* frame now. The conversation's no longer about fairness — it's about survival. You've got them working to justify why they deserve *you.*

Silence as the Kill Shot

After your counter, shut the fuck up. Don't fill the air with reasoning or charm. Let them flail. Silence is the chokehold of negotiation — invisible, slow, and absolute. They'll start second-guessing themselves, tweaking their own terms, promising more than you asked for. That's not luck. That's psychological gravity. When you hold the silence long enough, they collapse under it.

Bottom Line

You win the first move by refusing to make it. The fool talks; the predator listens. The moment you stay quiet, you seize control of the frame, the tempo, and the room. They think they're negotiating — but really, you're performing surgery. You're extracting truth, ego, and leverage in real time. By the time they realize what happened, you're already cashing the win.

Tactic 14.2:
Framing the Deal: Control Expectations, Feed Their Ego, Take It All

Negotiation isn't about facts. **It's about perception.** You don't win deals because you're offering the best terms—you win because you control how the other person *sees* those terms. This is called **framing the deal**, and it's the psychological equivalent of putting lipstick on a pig, convincing everyone it's a supermodel, and walking away with their wallet while they're still admiring the pig.

Here's the truth: People don't care about the objective value of a deal—they care about how it *feels*. And feelings are easy to manipulate. **Control the frame, and you control the outcome.** Make them think they're winning, stroke their ego just enough to keep them blind, and while they're busy patting themselves on the back, **you'll be walking away with everything that matters.**

1. The Power of Setting Expectations Early

The first impression isn't just important—it's **everything**. The way you present the deal from the start will shape how they view every detail after that.

- ◉ **Anchoring Bias:** People latch onto the first piece of information they hear. That's why you should set the bar **high or low** depending on what benefits you.

  - Selling something? *"This is top-tier, premium-level value."*

  - Buying something? *"We're looking at budget options here."*

- **Lowball the Situation:** Start by painting a bleak picture. *"Budgets are tight right now." "We've seen better offers elsewhere."* This lowers their expectations so when you *"reluctantly"* make a better offer, it feels like a win—even if it's exactly what you wanted from the start.

Pro Move: After setting low expectations, act like any slight improvement is a huge concession. *"Look, I normally wouldn't offer this, but for you..."*
Yeah, for them—because they're a sucker who just fell for it.

2. Feed Their Ego, Control Their Mind

People are driven by ego more than logic. **If you can make someone feel smart, powerful, or special, they'll agree to almost anything just to keep feeling that way.**

- **The "Expert" Trap:** Start by acknowledging their "expertise." *"You've clearly done your homework on this."* Now they're too busy feeling superior to realize they're getting played.

- **False Flattery:** Compliment them on something unrelated to the deal. *"You're sharp—I can tell you've got a great eye for this kind of thing."* Their brain associates you with positivity, making them less likely to argue.

- **The "Let Them Win" Trick:** Give them a meaningless victory early on. *"You're right about that small detail."* They'll feel like they're winning, making it easier for you to slip in the real terms without resistance.

3. The Illusion of Compromise: How to Make Them Think They're Winning

People hate feeling like they've been "sold." But they love feeling like they've **negotiated** a deal. So, give them that illusion—while you're actually taking everything.

- ◉ **The "High Anchor" Strategy:** Start with an offer that's intentionally outrageous. When they negotiate it down, they'll feel victorious, even though you've still landed exactly where you wanted.

  - Example: You want $10K. Start at $15K. When they "negotiate" you down to $10K, they feel like a genius. You feel like a wolf in a chicken coop.

- ◉ **Create Fake Trade-Offs:** Offer to "give up" things that don't matter to you but seem valuable to them.

  - *"Okay, I'll drop that fee—if you can agree to the timeline."*

  - Spoiler: That fee was never important. But now they think they've "won," while you've secured the real prize.

4. Control the Narrative, Control the Deal

You're not negotiating facts. **You're negotiating the story around those facts.**

- ◉ **Reframe the Weakness:** If they point out a flaw, flip it into a strength.

  - *"Sure, this isn't the cheapest option—but that's because it's the best."*

  - *"Yes, the timeline is tight—which means you'll see results faster."*

- ◉ **Never Defend—Redirect:** When challenged, don't argue. Just shift the focus.

  - *"Forget the price for a second—let's talk about the value you're getting here."*

- *"I hear your concern, but what's really important is how this will save you time in the long run."*

Bonus Move: When they start overthinking, overwhelm them with confidence. *"Look, you're overcomplicating this. Here's what matters…"* Then steamroll with your key point.

Negotiation isn't about being fair. It's about being first to control the frame. Set expectations low, feed their ego high, and create the illusion that they're winning. **Because when people think they've won, they stop looking for where they lost.** And by the time they figure it out? **You'll be long gone, deal in hand, with a smile that says, "Thanks for playing."**

Tactic 14.3:
Creating Urgency: Using Scarcity and Deadlines to Force Quick Deals

Urgency isn't negotiation—it's psychological torture disguised as progress. The minute you make someone believe time is running out, their logic goes on vacation and fear takes the wheel. Every "act now" pitch you've ever heard? That wasn't marketing. That was manipulation. The trick isn't to talk faster—it's to make *them* panic faster. You don't sell the deal; you sell the *clock* running out.

The Scarcity Hustle – Make Them Think It's Slipping Away

Scarcity is the oldest hustle in the book. You don't tell them what they're getting—you tell them what they're *about to lose.* People will crawl through broken glass to avoid loss, even if the thing they're losing is imaginary. You drop the line: "Only two left," or "I've got another buyer ready to sign." Lie? Maybe. Effective? Always. Their pulse spikes, their focus narrows, and now you own their emotional state.

Here's the punchline: it doesn't even have to be real scarcity. Half the time, there isn't another buyer, another slot, or another deal. There's just you—calm, collected, holding the illusion like a loaded gun while they sweat bullets trying not to miss out. You're not selling a product. You're selling the fear of regret. And fear is the fastest closer you'll ever meet.

The Deadline Trick – Give the Clock Teeth

Nothing breeds stupidity faster than a countdown. You slap an expiration date on a deal and suddenly grown adults start acting like toddlers trying to grab the last toy. "This price is only good until Friday." "I can only hold this number today." You say it like it's divine law written in smoke and lightning. It doesn't have to be true. The key is to make *them* believe the door is closing, right now, on *their* chance to win.

The beauty of a fake deadline? When they beg for an extension, you get to play savior. You sigh, act reluctant, pretend to "pull some strings," and then *graciously* offer them one last chance. They'll thank you while crawling deeper into your trap. You didn't sell a deal—you sold desperation wrapped in a clock.

The Phantom Competition – Fear of Missing Out on Nothing

Humans are addicted to rivalry. The moment they think someone else wants what they want, their survival wiring lights up. You don't need an actual competitor—you just need to sound like there is one. "I've got another call at noon from a guy ready to sign." "This slot might already be taken." It's vaporware with a heartbeat, and it drives people insane.

The second you invoke another buyer, the conversation stops being about price or value—it becomes a fight for validation. They'll start justifying *why* they deserve the deal, talking themselves right into your terms. You've made it emotional, not logical. And emotion will outspend logic every damn time.

Stack the Pressure – When One Trigger Isn't Enough

Want to break someone fast? Layer the triggers. Start with scarcity: "We've only got a few left." Add a deadline: "Offer expires Friday." Top it with competition: "I've got another party deciding tonight." That's a triple threat—fear, urgency, rivalry—all pulling at their nerves like piano wire.

Then, once they're sweating bullets, *pull back.* Go quiet. Smile. "Hey, no pressure. I totally get if you're not ready." That fake calm after the storm confuses the brain and seals the deal. They'll agree just to stop the internal chaos. You didn't negotiate —you induced a panic attack with a friendly tone.

The Aftermath – Make Panic Your Closer

Urgency isn't about making them act fast—it's about making them too scared to slow down. Scarcity tells them they're about to lose. Deadlines tell them time's running out. Competition tells them someone else is winning. Stack all three, and you've built a psychological chokehold that makes "no" impossible.

When you control the clock, you control the mind. And once you've got their mind, the deal's already yours.

> *The first voice in a negotiation isn't the leader—it's the sacrifice. You don't rush to speak; you wait for them to bleed information. Every word they spill is a wound you'll reopen later. The quiet man runs the room because everyone else is desperate to fill his silence. That's not strategy. That's predation.*

Lesson 15: Psychological Pressure–Making the Other Side Crack

Tactic 15.1:
The Psychological Chokehold: Weaponizing Time & Silence

Silence isn't awkward. It's a fucking weapon. Time isn't patience. It's pressure. You don't need to shout, threaten, or argue when you can just sit there and let the other person rot in their own discomfort. That's the chokehold — slow, invisible, and deadly. When you learn to control silence and time, you don't negotiate anymore. You *own* people. You make them beg to end the tension you built by simply shutting the fuck up.

The Power of Predatory Silence – Shut Up and Let Them Break

Most amateurs can't handle silence because they equate noise with control. They think talking keeps them in charge. Wrong. Every word you say is a leak in your armor. Every pause you hold is a hand around their throat. You stop talking, and their brain starts eating itself alive. "Did I say something wrong?" "Are they mad?" "Are they still interested?" You can *hear* their insecurity start breathing heavy.

When you go quiet, don't flinch. Don't nod, don't smile, don't fill the space. Just *exist*. Let the air get heavy. You'll see it happen — they'll start negotiating against themselves just to break the silence. They'll raise their own offer, justify their own mistakes, or backpedal without you saying a word. The silence isn't empty; it's loaded. It's the sound of you owning the room without lifting a finger.

Time as a Weapon – Drag It Out Until They Snap

Patience is power. Time is control. The longer you make someone wait, the weaker they become. Every day that passes without a response makes them a little more desperate. They start wondering what went wrong, replaying every word, questioning every decision. You didn't reject them — you *let them stew.* That's worse. Silence leaves space for imagination, and imagination always paints darker pictures than reality.

You want to see panic? Ignore a follow-up email. Skip a scheduled call. Let them twist in uncertainty. Then, when you finally respond, act like it's no big deal. "Hey, been busy. What's up?" That dismissive tone crushes them. You're not the one chasing; they are. You've flipped the script. They're now begging for closure, for reassurance, for *anything* that makes the pressure stop.

Deadlines mean nothing to you. When they say, "We need an answer by Friday," you say, "We'll see." Let Friday come and go. Let them feel the weight of their own deadline. The silence after their imaginary clock runs out will break them faster than any argument ever could.

The Ghost Move – Vanish and Let Them Lose Their Mind

Sometimes you don't need to delay — you need to disappear. Mid-negotiation, mid-conversation, just vanish. Don't text, don't call, don't explain. Ghost them cold. People are addicted to patterns, and when you break the rhythm, they lose their grip. The absence of your voice becomes louder than anything you could've said.

Then, when you resurface days later, pretend like nothing happened. "Hey, just checking back in." They'll pretend they weren't panicking, but you'll see it in their tone — softer, more agreeable, ready to make a deal just to get you back. You've taught them one thing: your silence is scarier than your words.

The Mindfuck of Unpredictability – Control by Chaos

The chokehold works best when they can't predict you. Speak, then stop. Promise, then delay. Respond once, then vanish. It's not randomness — it's control. You're conditioning them to chase clarity from you, because clarity feels like oxygen after you've strangled them with uncertainty. Every pause, every delay, every late reply turns you into the drug they can't quit.

When they get emotional, you stay ice-cold. They'll yell, argue, guilt-trip — you sit there like you're watching a bad sitcom. "I prefer to take my time." That one line hits harder than any insult. You just told them they don't control the pace — *you do.*

The Aftermath – When Nothing Becomes Everything

Silence isn't passive. It's domination without noise. Time isn't waiting. It's strangulation by patience. You don't fight. You don't argue. You let the clock do your dirty work. Every second of uncertainty is a blade you twist deeper without ever moving your hand.

The weak fill silence because they can't stand what it says. The powerful weaponize it because they know exactly what it does. So next time someone tries to rush you, drown them in quiet. The longer they wait, the louder their panic gets — and by the time they open their mouth to break it, they've already lost.

Tactic 15.2:
Pre-Win Dominance: How to Make Them Sell Themselves to You

You don't need dirty tricks to win. You need two things: a spine made of steel and preparation that makes other people feel like they have to prove they're worth your time. Pre-Win Positioning isn't about lying or breaking people down — it's about walking into the room with real leverage and making them show you why you should care. Do this right and they'll spend the meeting convincing *you* they're the right choice. That's power that doesn't require dishonesty, only ruthless clarity.

Own the Room Before You Speak — Presence Is a Promise

When you walk in, act like you already have options. Not because you're bluffing, but because you're prepared. Posture, tone, and timing translate into perceived value. Don't fawn, don't apologize for being there. Say what you need to say, once, with authority. People will immediately calibrate toward you and pitch to your standard because humans instinctively measure value against perceived scarcity and confidence.

Do the basic shit right: be on time, have a clean brief, know their names and titles, and arrive with a clear non-negotiable outline of what success looks like. That quiet competence speaks louder than rhetoric. You don't have to be loud — you have to be unmistakable.

The Reverse Pitch — Make Them Tell You Why They Matter

Stop selling. Start asking the right questions and make them sell themselves. Instead of presenting a long list of benefits, throw the spotlight on them:

"Tell me why you think you're the one for this."

"What makes your approach different from everyone else I've seen?"

They'll scramble to deliver proof, to justify, to position their value. The difference between a good and bad pitch is how much the presenter can make the listener *believe*—and when the listener is you, they'll work harder. You're not being cruel; you're doing your job as a buyer of talent/value: vetting, probing, extracting truth.

Take notes like you don't believe them yet. That silence after their answer forces clarity. They'll either step up with specifics or collapse into vagueness — and you'll know which one to trust.

Plant Seeds of Doubt — But Be Honest About It

You want them to improve their offer? Make them see the gap without fabricating drama. Ask pointed, evidence-based questions that expose weak spots:

"You mentioned X. How do you measure success on that?"
"This sounds expensive. What exactly goes into that cost?"

These questions are not tricks — they're due diligence. If their answers are strong, you gain real confidence. If they're weak, they'll either fix it on the spot or you'll have your reason to pass. Do not invent threats or fake competitors. Use real standards, timelines, and benchmarks. That keeps you ethical and immovable.

The Calm Evaluate — Listen, Judge, Don't Plead

While they talk, be detached — not rude, but clinical. Nod when it's good, ask for clarification when it's thin. Take up the mental posture of an evaluator, not a supplicant. People perform when being assessed. Make your posture, your note-taking, and your questions communicate that you're weighing them, not begging them.

If they make a bold claim, ask for proof. If they promise an outcome, ask for metrics. Get commitments on timelines and deliverables. The more concrete they get, the more they've sold you — voluntarily.

Walk-Away Integrity — Your Best Card

The moment you *need* the deal, you lose leverage. Your calm walk-away is the real power move. But you can't fake it: walking away only works if you mean it. That doesn't mean you're petty — it means you respect your time and standards. Say it plainly:

"If this isn't aligned with the outcomes we agreed, this isn't going to work for me."

Then pause. Give them the space to counter with substance, not emotion. If they come back with better terms, great. If not, you save your energy and reputation for better fights.nWalking away ethically also preserves relationships — you leave room for future talks on different terms instead of burning bridges with drama.

Force Them to Commit to the Concrete — No Vagaries

Vagueness is the enemy of deals. When they offer concepts, force specifics: price, delivery, milestones, KPIs, accountability. Ask for the exact person who will be responsible, the exact toolset they'll use, the exact dates. Once something is concrete, it's either a commitment or a lie — and you can act on that.

You win when what's on the table can be measured. You lose when everyone's agreeing to "trust" and "collaboration" without metrics.

Finish Like a Pro — Clear Next Steps, Clear Pressure

End the meeting with a concise recap and a firm timeline:

"Great. Here's what I need to see by Friday: X, Y, Z. If that's in place, we'll move forward on these terms. If not, we'll pause."

That clarity is both a courtesy and leverage. It frames the next move as theirs to execute. It makes the negotiation a process, not a drama. Follow up exactly as promised — trustworthy follow-through wins more long term than theatrics.

Enhanced Tactics

1. Walk In Like You Own the Fucking Room (Because You Do)

Confidence isn't optional—it's the currency of dominance. People don't question the guy who acts like he's already won. They start second-guessing themselves instead.

- ◉ **The "Assumed Authority" Move:**
  Walk into any negotiation with the mindset that you're doing *them* a favor by even showing up.

  - *"Let's see if this makes sense for me."*

  - *"I don't commit unless it's exactly what I need."*
    Translation: *"You're lucky I'm even here."*

- ◉ **Set the Frame Early:**

  - *"I'm selective about who I work with."*

  - *"I'm not sure this is the right fit for me, but let's find out."*

  This flips the script—they're no longer evaluating you. **They're trying to prove they're worthy of you.**

- ◉ **Bonus Move: Deliberately misinterpret their importance.**

  - *"Remind me what your role is again?"*
    It's a subtle, dismissive jab that makes them feel like they've got to work harder to impress you.

2. The Reverse Pitch: Make Them Sell Themselves

Why sell when you can get them to do it for you? People love talking about themselves—**use that weakness against them.**

- ◉ **Lead with Questions, Not Statements:**
  Instead of pitching your value, **make them pitch why they're valuable to you.**

  - *"Why should I choose to work with you?"*

  - *"What makes you different from the others I've talked to?"*

Now they're scrambling to justify their worth, and every word they say puts you in a stronger position.

- **The "Silent Evaluation" Trick:**
  After they answer, **say nothing.** Just nod slowly, maybe jot down a note like you're unimpressed.
  That silence is a vacuum they'll desperately try to fill with more selling points—**and more concessions.**

- **Bonus Move:** When they ask about *your* side, respond with:

  - *"I don't need to sell myself—I'm selective, and that speaks for itself."*

  It's a cocky move, but it'll rattle anyone desperate to close the deal.

3. Plant the Seed of Insecurity: Make Them Chase Validation

People crave validation, especially in high-stakes situations. **Your job? Dangle that validation like a carrot they'll never quite reach.**

- **The Backhanded Compliment:**

  - *"You've got an interesting approach—not sure it's the best, but interesting."*

  It's a psychological grenade: part praise, part insult. They'll spend the rest of the meeting trying to "prove" themselves.

- **Subtle Indifference:**
  Show zero emotional reaction to their big selling points.

  - *"Okay."*

  - *"Noted."*

The lack of excitement makes them feel like they haven't done enough—so they'll keep trying harder, offering more.

- ◉ **Bonus Move:**
  End a strong pitch from them with:

  - *"I'll have to think about it."*
    That one line? **It's a mindfuck.** They'll obsess over it, replaying the conversation in their head, wondering what they did wrong—and what they can do to fix it.

4. The "Deal Reversal" Tactic: Make Them Think It's Their Loss If You Walk

The final nail in their psychological coffin is making them believe **they need you more than you need them**—even if that's total bullshit.

- ◉ **The Fake Flinch:**
  Right when they think they've got you, **act hesitant.**

  - *"I'm not sure this is worth my time."*

  - *"I thought this would be more aligned with what I need."*

  Suddenly, **they're the ones begging you to stay in the deal.**

- ◉ **The Walk-Away Threat (Without Actually Leaving):**

  - *"Maybe this isn't the right fit after all."*
    Then **pause.** Let the tension hang.

  Watch them scramble to pull you back in, offering better terms without you even asking.

- ◉ **Bonus Move:**
  If they *do* push back, hit them with:

- *"Look, I'm not here to convince you—I don't need to."*

That's the final power move. It says: **"I win, whether you realize it or not."**

Bottom Line

Pre-Win Dominance isn't about negotiating—it's about making them negotiate with themselves. You create an environment where they're so busy trying to impress you, they don't realize you're the one pulling the strings. **Confidence, indifference, and psychological manipulation are your weapons.**

And the best part? **You don't even have to try that hard—just sit back, let them talk, and watch them sell you on a deal you've already fucking won.**

Tactic 15.3:
Emotional Triggers & Fear Tactics: Breaking Them Without Saying a Word

You've got them sitting across the table, thinking it's just a negotiation. **Wrong.** It's a fucking psychological battlefield—and while they're armed with logic and polite corporate bullshit, **you're holding a loaded gun called fear.**

Here's the truth: **People don't make decisions based on facts.** They make decisions based on fear—fear of losing, fear of looking stupid, fear of regret, fear of missing out. **Your job? Push every one of those fucking buttons until they're too rattled to think straight.** This isn't about being fair. **It's about breaking their emotional spine so they fold faster than cheap lawn furniture.**

1. The Fear of Loss: The Ultimate Mindfuck

Loss hurts more than winning feels good. This isn't some motivational quote—it's science. Humans are wired to avoid loss at all costs. **So, create the illusion that they're about to lose everything.**

- ◉ **The "Almost Gone" Gambit:**
  Make them think the deal is slipping through their fingers.

  - *"We've got another party interested, and they're moving faster."*

  - *"I was excited about this, but I'm starting to reconsider."*

  Just enough to make them panic, but not enough to let them walk away. **You want them dangling on the edge.**

- ◉ **Scarcity Without Scarcity:**
  Even if there's **no one else in the game,** act like there is.

  - *"We're finalizing things soon—I'd hate for you to miss out."*
    Translation: *"You're not as special as you think you are."*

  That fear of being left out? It'll have them agreeing to terms they swore they'd never accept.

- ◉ **Bonus Move:**
  Say nothing after dropping the threat of loss. **Silence amplifies fear.** They'll fill the void with concessions.

2. Triggering Insecurity: Make Them Doubt Themselves

Confidence is fragile. Even the cockiest asshole has a crack somewhere. **Your job? Find it. Smash it. Exploit it.**

- ◉ **The Subtle Undercut:**
  Compliment them—**then twist the knife.**

  - *"You've got a solid team, though I'm surprised at some of the decisions here."*

- *"You clearly know your stuff... but this part feels rushed."*
  Translation: *"You're not as smart as you think you are."*

They'll scramble to prove you wrong, which means **they'll start over-explaining, over-compensating, and —most importantly—offering more.**

- ◉ **Doubt by Comparison:**

  - *"I've worked with others in your position who approached this differently."*
    Now they're thinking: *"Am I doing something wrong? Am I missing something?"*
    That insecurity? **It's leverage.**

- ◉ **Bonus Move:**
  After they make a point, respond with:

  - *"Hmm. Interesting perspective."*
    That's it. No validation. No agreement. Just enough to make them question themselves.

3. The Guilt Trip: Make Them Feel Like They Owe You

Guilt is a powerful motivator. **You don't even have to say much —just create the illusion that they've let you down.**

- ◉ **The "Disappointed but Not Angry" Act:**

  - *"I really thought we were on the same page here."*

  - *"I was hoping for a more serious offer."*
    That subtle disappointment? It hits harder than anger because **now they feel responsible for fixing it.**

- ◉ **Make It Personal:**
  Even if it's business, frame it like they've crossed a personal line.

  - *"I've invested a lot of time in this because I believed in it."*

Now they feel like they owe you something—even if they don't.

- ◉ **Bonus Move:**
  End with:

  - *"I expected more from you."*
  Boom. Now they're negotiating with their own guilt, not with you.

4. The Fear of Making a Mistake: The Decision Freeze

People fear making the wrong choice more than anything. **You can weaponize that fear until they're too scared to walk away from the deal.**

- ◉ **Highlight the Risk of Saying "No":**

  - *"Are you sure you're comfortable passing on this opportunity? Because once it's gone, it's gone."*

  - *"I'd hate for you to look back and realize this was the one you missed."*
  That fear of future regret? **It's paralyzing.**

- ◉ **The "What If" Trap:**
  Plant a seed of doubt they can't ignore.

  - *"What if someone else takes this and it turns out to be huge?"*
  Now their brain is stuck on that *"what if,"* making them afraid to walk away.

- ◉ **Bonus Move:**
  After laying out the fear, **go silent.**
  Their brain will fill the gap with worst-case scenarios—and by the time they open their mouth again, they'll be ready to sign whatever the fuck you put in front of them.

Bottom Line

Negotiation isn't about logic. It's about emotions. Fear, insecurity, guilt, and regret are the levers you pull to make people crumble. **You don't argue. You don't convince. You just press the right psychological buttons until they break.**

This isn't persuasion—it's psychological warfare.
And when done right? **They'll thank you for it.**

Tactic 15.4.:
The Power of Walking Away: How Small Losses Win Big Wars

Here's the fucking truth most people can't handle: The strongest move you can make in any negotiation is to get up, flip the proverbial table (or the literal one, if you've got the balls), and **walk the fuck away.** Not with a polite, "Well, thank you for your time" bullshit smile. No. **Walk away like you've just wasted precious minutes of your life dealing with idiots.** Because here's the thing—**desperation reeks, and people can smell it from a mile away.**

You want power? Stop clinging to deals like a broke-ass ex who can't take a hint. **You don't need them—they need you.** And when you act like it, they'll start chasing you like lost puppies, begging to get back to the table. It's psychological warfare 101: **the moment you're willing to lose, you've already fucking won.** Because nothing scares the shit out of people more than realizing you're not afraid to leave them—and their weak-ass offer—behind.

1. The "Fuck You" Factor: Why Walking Away Is the Ultimate Power Move

When you walk away, **you're not losing a deal—you're sending a message:**

"I don't need your crumbs. I'll burn this bridge and light my cigar with the flames."

- ◉ **It Shatters Their Ego:** People expect you to fight, to compromise, to beg. When you just stand up and say, *"Nah, I'm good,"* it fucks with their head.

- ◉ **It Creates Scarcity:** Suddenly, *you* are the limited resource. You're the deal they can't have, the opportunity slipping through their desperate little fingers.

- ◉ **Bonus Move:** Don't just walk away—**leave something hanging.**

  - *"I thought you were smarter than this. Guess I was wrong."*
  Then walk. No looking back. They'll be replaying that line in their head for days, wondering how they fucked up.

2. How to Weaponize Loss: Sacrifice Small to Win Big

Most people cling to every deal like it's life or death. **That's weak.** Real power comes from knowing when to say, *"Fuck it. Keep your scraps."* Sometimes, losing on purpose sets you up to win bigger down the line.

- ◉ **The Strategic Loss:** Walk away from a small deal to make them desperate for the next one.

  - *"If you're not ready to meet serious terms, I've got better shit to do."*
  Now they're thinking, *"Wait, what did I miss? Was this bigger than I thought?"*

- ◉ **Make Them Feel It:** After walking away, let them stew. No follow-up emails. No calls. **Just silence.**
  The absence of your presence will eat at them like a bad case of guilt mixed with insecurity.

- ◉ **Bonus Move:** When they finally crawl back, act like you're doing *them* a favor by even considering it.

  - *"Oh, you're still interested? I've moved on, but let's see if it's even worth my time now."*

3. The "Chase Me, Bitch" Effect: Making Them Work for You

Walking away flips the script. **Now they're chasing you.** Why? Because people want what they can't have—and nothing screams "unattainable" like someone who couldn't give less of a fuck.

- ◉ **Reverse the Desperation:**

  - While they're busy overthinking where they went wrong, you're living rent-free in their head.

  - *"We were close to a deal, but you clearly don't understand value. Good luck with that."*
    Then vanish. Watch how fast they come crawling back, suddenly *understanding* your value.

- ◉ **Control the Re-Entry:**
  When they do reach out, don't respond right away. Let them sweat. When you finally reply, keep it short. No enthusiasm. No excitement. Just:

  - *"I'm busy. Maybe next week."*
    Now they're dancing to your tune—and **you didn't even have to play the fucking music.**

4. Walk Away Like You Mean It

Here's the catch: **You can't fake this shit.** If you threaten to walk but don't mean it, they'll see through you faster than a cheap knockoff. You've got to believe, deep in your core, that you're better off without them. And if you don't? **You've already lost.**

- **No Apologies, No Explanations:**
  Don't explain why you're walking. **Just walk.** The more you talk, the weaker you sound.

- **Own the Room, Even on Your Way Out:**
  Stand tall, hold your ground, and leave like you've got better places to be—because you fucking do.

Walking away isn't the last resort. It's the ultimate power move. It's the middle finger of negotiation—the boldest way to say, *"I don't need you. You need me."* And when you walk away with that kind of unapologetic, zero-fucks energy, you'll find people chasing you down, begging to give you what you wanted in the first place.

Because in the end, the person who's willing to lose is the one who always fucking wins.

Tactic 15.5:
Creating Dependency: How to Build Long-Term Influence They Can't Escape

You want real power? Not just one-off wins or temporary control—**I'm talking about psychological handcuffs that people willingly slap on themselves.** The kind of influence where even if they walk away, they'll crawl back eventually because you've embedded yourself in their mind like a parasite they can't shake. **That's dependency.**

You don't build this shit overnight. **It's the long con.** You make them think they're in charge, all while tightening the invisible leash around their neck. The best part? **They'll thank you for it.** They won't even realize they're addicted until it's too late. Like emotional crack, they'll keep coming back for more—**and you'll be the only dealer in town.**

1. The Hook: Make Them Need You Without Realizing It

Dependency starts with one simple trick: **give them just enough to think they're winning, but never enough to feel secure.** Keep the carrot dangling just out of reach, and they'll chase it forever.

- **Create Micro Wins:** Let them "win" small battles that mean jack shit to you.

  - *"You're right, we'll adjust that tiny detail."* (Translation: I don't give a fuck, but now you feel smart.)

- **Drip Feed Validation:** Praise them just enough to keep them hooked.

  - *"I've never worked with someone as sharp as you."*— then pull back and go cold for a few days. Watch them spiral, wondering what they did wrong.

- **Bonus Move:** When they start to feel confident, shake the ground beneath them.

  - *"You're getting there."* Just those three words can make someone question everything.

2. Build the Habit: Make Them Rely on You for Decisions

You don't just want their attention—you want to be the voice in their head. **The goal? Make them incapable of making decisions without your approval.**

- **Ask Leading Questions:**

  - *"What do you think the best option is here?"*—then subtly guide them to *your* conclusion.

  - *"Do you really think that's the best approach?"*—plant doubt, then swoop in with your "solution."

- ◉ **Control the Flow of Information:**

  - Feed them selective facts that reinforce your position. **Information is power, and you control the drip.**

- ◉ **The Dependency Loop:**

  - Give advice → they follow it → they succeed → they credit *you* → repeat until they can't function without your input.

3. Create the Fear of Loss: Make Them Afraid to Lose You

Nothing cements dependency like fear. **People are more motivated by the fear of losing something than the joy of gaining it.** So, become the thing they're terrified to lose.

- ◉ **Occasional Disappearances:**

  - Ghost them unexpectedly. No explanations. When you return, act like nothing happened. It creates anxiety and makes them realize how much they depend on your presence.

- ◉ **The Scarcity Play:**

  - *"I've been really busy with other projects."* Translation: *"You're not my priority anymore."* Watch them scramble to win you back.

- ◉ **Emotional Withdrawal:**

  - When they get too comfortable, pull the rug out:

    - ✓ *"I'm not sure this is working as well as I thought."*

    - ✓ That one line will keep them awake at night, replaying every interaction, desperate to "fix" it.

4. Make Yourself Irreplaceable (Even If You're Not)

The final nail in the dependency coffin? **Convince them there's no one else like you.** They could try to walk away, but good luck finding someone who fucks with their head like you do.

- **Be the Solution to Every Problem:**
  Even if you caused the problem in the first place, be the one who "fixes" it.

  - *"That's tricky—I've dealt with this before. Here's what I'd do."*

- **Subtle Undermining:**

  - Casually point out how others don't measure up:

    - ✓ *"I'm surprised they handled it that way. I'd have approached it differently."*
      Now, every time they deal with someone else, they'll hear *your* voice in the back of their mind.

- **Bonus Move:** End conversations on your terms. Always.

  - *"I've got to run, but we'll pick this up later."*—like *you're* the busy one, even if you're just going to sit on your ass scrolling your phone.

Dependency isn't built with chains—it's built with invisible strings. You don't force people to rely on you; you let them *think* it's their choice. Control the wins, manage the information, disappear just enough to keep them anxious, and always leave them wanting more. **Because the ultimate power isn't having someone's attention—it's owning their fucking mind.**

You don't win by talking louder. You win by letting the silence rot their confidence from the inside out. Every second you wait is another crack in their armor. Patience isn't virtue—it's violence done slowly. When they start negotiating against themselves just to make the pressure stop, that's not compromise. That's collapse.

Chapter Aftermath

You didn't make a deal—you made a *mindfuck*. Every tactic in this chapter wasn't about talking terms. It was about rewriting reality while they thought they were in control. You let them speak first so they'd bleed information. You let them think they were leading while you quietly dismantled their position piece by piece. You didn't sell a product—you sold *desperation*. And they bought it, thinking it was a win.

That's the dirty secret of negotiation: it's not a dance. It's a dismantling. You're not finding common ground—you're feeding their ego just enough to keep them blind while you loot the goddamn castle. Time, silence, pressure—those aren't tools. They're *weapons*. And when you stack them right, the other side folds themselves without ever knowing they were played.

They didn't walk away with a win. They walked away relieved. And that's how you know you broke them. You didn't just negotiate—you *conquered*.

CHAPTER SEVEN

Psych Warfare in Power Dynamics

Welcome to Chapter 7, the motherfucking battlefield where power isn't earned—it's taken. This chapter isn't for the faint of heart or the weak-minded. It's for those who understand that real influence isn't about charm or charisma; it's about control, fear, and manipulation. Here, we rip the mask off the sanitized bullshit of corporate etiquette and polite negotiations to reveal the raw, ruthless strategies that dominate boardrooms, courtrooms, and every goddamn room in between.

Chapter 7 is your war manual, packed with lessons that expose the brutal truths behind mental manipulation, strategic control, and psychological defense. It's not about playing fair; it's about playing smart, dirty, and without a shred of remorse. Each lesson is designed to sharpen your mind like a weapon, teaching you how to identify, exploit, and dismantle threats before they even know they're in your crosshairs.

Lesson 16: The Art of Mental Manipulation

Tactic 16.1:
The Power of Perception: Reality Is for Suckers

The truth doesn't matter if you can sell a better lie. That's the brutal, reality of psychological warfare. People don't give a damn about facts—they believe what *feels* true, what's repeated enough times, and what's delivered with unshakeable confidence. Perception isn't just reality; it's the loaded gun you aim at anyone too naive, too lazy, or too trusting to question it. In a world where information overload makes everyone a surface-level thinker, the loudest voice wins—not the most honest one.

History isn't written by the honest; it's written by the winners. And those winners didn't get there by playing nice or sticking to the facts. They got there by controlling the story. It doesn't matter if the truth is buried somewhere underneath a pile of crap —what matters is what people *believe*. You don't need to be the smartest person in the room; you just need to be the one holding the microphone. Shout your version of reality loud enough, often enough, and even the people who *know* it's B.S. will start to doubt themselves. That's the power of perception: it rewrites reality without changing a single fact.

So, how do you weaponize perception like a goddamn professional? Here's the blueprint:

- **Own the Narrative:** Don't defend. Don't explain. Don't justify. Speak with absolute conviction, even if you're full of shit. Confidence beats facts every single time. When you act like your version is the gospel, people fall in line because questioning you requires more effort than agreeing with you.

- **Repeat Until It's Reality:** Repetition is brainwashing with a polite face. Say it. Say it again. Then say it some more.

The more often people hear something, the more likely they are to believe it—no matter how absurd it sounds.

- **Reframe the Situation:** You don't need to argue over facts when you can reframe them. Turn mistakes into "strategic decisions," failures into "learning experiences," and blatant lies into "alternative perspectives." It's not what happened; it's how you *present* what happened.

- **Make People Doubt Themselves:** When someone challenges your version of reality, flip the script: *"Are you sure you understand it correctly?"* Plant that seed of doubt. Make them second-guess their own memory, their own logic. It's psychological quicksand—once they start sinking, they're fucked.

Want to ruin someone? Don't attack their actions. Attack how people *perceive* their actions. Turn a confident leader into an arrogant asshole with just the right spin. Make a passionate advocate look like an unhinged lunatic. It's not about what they did; it's about how you *frame* what they did. The beauty of it? You don't even need to lie. Just twist the truth until it screams.

Bottom line? Reality is for suckers. Perception is where the power lives. Control perception, and you don't just win the battle —you make sure no one even realizes there was a battle in the first place. That's not manipulation. That's mastery.

Tactic 16.2:
Emotional Leverage: Making People Dance to Your Tune

Power isn't about brute force—it's about control. And the easiest way to control someone isn't through threats or logic; it's through their emotions. People think they make rational decisions, but they don't. They react based on fear, insecurity, pride, and desire. If you know how to pull those strings, you can make them move however the fuck you want.

Think of emotions like a control panel—push the right button, and people act without thinking. Want loyalty? Trigger guilt. Want obedience? Create fear. Need them to self-destruct? Stoke their insecurities. Once you understand what drives someone, you don't have to convince them to do anything—you make them *feel* like it was their idea. That's not persuasion. That's dominance.

Here's how to turn emotions into weapons:

- **Guilt as a Chain:** People hate feeling like they owe a debt—especially one they can't repay. Remind them of favors, generosity, or sacrifices you've made. "After everything I've done for you…" is enough to keep them in check. If they resist, double down. "I guess loyalty doesn't mean shit to you." Watch them cave.

- **Fear as a Leash:** The easiest way to control someone is to make them afraid. Fear of losing money, status, relationships—it doesn't matter. Subtly remind them what's at stake. "I wouldn't want this to get out…" or "You sure you want to risk that?" Fear makes people compliant.

- **Insecurity as a Weapon:** Find their weakness and exploit it. Everyone's afraid of being exposed as incompetent, unworthy, or replaceable. Drop hints that they're slipping, that others are questioning them. "I'm hearing things… but I'm sure it's nothing." Make them paranoid. Make them scramble to prove themselves—to *you.*

- **Anger as a Distraction:** People make the dumbest mistakes when they're pissed off. If someone is standing in your way, push their buttons. Insult their intelligence, question their integrity, laugh at their beliefs. Once they react emotionally, they're playing *your* game, not theirs.

People like to believe they're in control of their emotions. They're not. Most are just puppets waiting for the right strings to be pulled. You don't need to force them to do shit—just make them *feel* like they have no other choice. That's how real power works.

Bottom line? Logic doesn't move people—emotions do. If you know which buttons to push, you don't just influence behavior—you own it.

Tactic 16.3:
Manufactured Chaos: Creating Problems Only You Can Solve

People crave stability, but nothing grants power faster than controlled chaos. When people feel overwhelmed, uncertain, or desperate, they look for someone to take control. That's where you come in. You don't solve problems—you *create* them, then position yourself as the only one who can fix the mess. That's not deception. That's strategic fucking genius.

The trick is making sure the chaos looks natural, unavoidable, or someone else's fault. If you're caught, you're the villain. But if you do it right, people will beg for your help without realizing you're the one who set the fire in the first place.

Here's how to turn chaos into control:

- **Misdirection:** People fear uncertainty more than reality. Plant multiple problems at once—something obvious to keep them distracted and something subtle to make them uneasy. If they're panicked about one issue, they won't notice the real manipulation happening elsewhere.

- **Create Dependency:** If they trust you to solve problems, they'll never question if you caused them. Let them believe they're just "lucky" you were around when things went wrong. Soon enough, they won't make a move without your approval.

- **Destroy and Rebuild:** Break systems, processes, or relationships—but not all at once. Slowly introduce problems, let them struggle, then swoop in with *your* solution. They'll be grateful, unaware that they've just handed you control.

- **Amplify Small Problems:** A minor inconvenience can be turned into a full-blown disaster with the right spin. Use selective information, escalate the urgency, and watch them spiral. "If this doesn't get handled *now*, the whole thing could collapse." Fear makes people reckless. Guide them toward *your* outcome.

People don't want to think—they want someone to tell them what to do. Manufactured chaos makes that decision easy. They'll see you as the savior, not realizing you built the crisis in the first place. And when someone controls both the disease *and* the cure, they don't just hold power—they *own* it.

Bottom line? If stability gives others control, then chaos gives it back to you. Create the problem, control the solution, and make damn sure they never see your fingerprints on either.

Tactic 16.4:
Gaslighting 2.0: Rewriting Reality Like a Pro

Reality isn't fixed—it's negotiable. If you control someone's perception, you control their entire world. That's where gaslighting comes in. This isn't just about making someone doubt their memory—it's about systematically breaking down their confidence, replacing their version of reality with yours, and ensuring they *thank you* for the privilege. Gaslighting isn't manipulation. It's mind control in its purest fucking form.

Most people think gaslighting is just lying, but it's much more than that. It's about making them question what they *know* to be true until they rely on you to tell them what's real. Done right, they won't just believe you—they'll defend you against anyone who says otherwise. They'll *need* you, because without you, their world won't make sense. That's power.

Here's how to rewrite reality like a pro:

- **Deny, Deny, Deny:** No matter what they say, no matter how much proof they think they have, flat-out deny it. "That never happened." "You're imagining things." "You're overreacting." Say it with conviction, and they'll start doubting themselves before they doubt you.

- **Contradict Subtly:** If you change the story too drastically, they'll resist. Instead, shift details just enough to make them question themselves. "I never said that— what I actually said was…" Small corrections lead to big doubts.

- **Use Their Emotions Against Them:** Make them feel irrational for even questioning you. "You're being paranoid." "You're always so sensitive." Turn their frustration into guilt, making them hesitant to challenge you again.

- **Isolate and Reinforce:** Gaslighting works best when you control their environment. Limit their exposure to outside opinions. "Nobody else has a problem with this." "They don't know what they're talking about." If you're their only reliable source, your version of reality *becomes* reality.

The beauty of gaslighting is that once they start relying on you for the truth, you own them. They won't trust their own mind, their own memories, or their own instincts. And when that happens, they'll never question you again.

Bottom line? Reality is whatever you say it is. Make them doubt themselves, make them trust you, and by the time they realize what's happening—if they ever do—it's already too late.

Perception isn't just power—it's prophecy. Control what people think they see, and they'll rewrite the truth for you. You don't argue with reality—you replace it. Every confident lie becomes history, every well-timed silence becomes proof. The world doesn't reward truth-tellers; it worships great storytellers who never blink.

Lesson 17: Tactical Control: Strategic Sabotage

Tactic 17.1:
The Puppet Master Strategy: Pulling Strings from the Shadows

Real power isn't about being in the spotlight—it's about controlling the people who are. The smartest motherfuckers in the game don't need to be the boss, the CEO, or the face of an operation. They just need to be the one whispering in the right ears, pushing the right buttons, and making the decisions without ever taking the heat. When you master the art of pulling strings from the shadows, you control everything, and no one even knows it.

True puppet masters don't demand power. They make others *want* to give it to them. People like to believe they're in charge, so let them. Let them take the credit, the responsibility, the blame—while you quietly shape every outcome to benefit *you*. You're not looking for titles; you're looking for influence.

Here's how to control people without them realizing it:

- **Make Them Feel in Control:** No one likes to feel manipulated, so don't let them. Instead, guide them toward your preferred outcome while making them believe it was their idea. "That's a great plan—you know what would make it even better?" Now they're doing exactly what you want, thinking it's their own genius at work.

- **Feed Their Ego:** People are slaves to their vanity. Praise their intelligence, their leadership, their instincts —just enough to make them crave your validation. The more they rely on your approval, the more influence you have.

- **Be the 'Trusted Advisor':** The person in power rarely makes decisions alone. They have confidants, advisors, and inner circles. Position yourself as the one they turn to when shit gets complicated. Once you're the source of their information, you dictate what they see, what they think, and what they do.

- **Create Subtle Dependency:** Give just enough insight, guidance, or support that they start depending on you. But never give them *everything*—leave just enough doubt that they keep coming back for more. Make them feel like without you, they'd be lost.

The best manipulators don't fight for control; they convince others to hand it over willingly. You don't need the title, the office, or the authority—you just need the right person under your influence. When the real decisions are being made, you'll be the one making them, even if your nam never comes up.

Bottom line? Power is an illusion. The trick is letting people *think* they have it while you're the one calling the fucking shots.

Tactic 17.2:
The Fear Factor: Making People Obey Without Question

Fear is the oldest and most effective tool of control. It's stronger than logic, more reliable than persuasion, and cheaper than loyalty. When people are scared, they don't think—they react. They don't resist—they comply. The key to absolute control isn't respect or admiration—it's making damn sure that the thought of going against you terrifies them.

Fear doesn't mean screaming threats like some amateur. That shit wears off. Real fear is subtle. It's the unspoken understanding that stepping out of line will have consequences. When people believe that defying you could cost them something—money, status, reputation, security—they don't fight back. They don't even *consider* it.

Here's how to weaponize fear without looking like a tyrant:

- **Establish Consequences Early:** If someone crosses you, *make an example out of them*. Not just for their sake, but for everyone watching. "Did you hear what happened to the last guy who tried that?" That's the kind of sentence that keeps people in line.

- **Keep People Uncertain:** Predictability breeds comfort. You don't want that. Make sure people can't anticipate your moves. Keep them wondering what might set you off, what might happen if they push too far. Fear thrives in uncertainty.

- **Use Silence as a Threat:** You don't always need to react. Sometimes, just going cold—ignoring someone, delaying a response—makes them spiral into anxiety. "Are they mad? Am I in trouble?" Let their own imagination do the heavy lifting.

- **Control Their Weak Points:** Everyone has something they're afraid of losing. A job, a relationship, a reputation. Find it. Make sure they *know* you could take it away—but never say it outright. "You wouldn't want this to become a problem, would you?" Let them connect the dots.

- **Reward Fearful Obedience:** Fear alone isn't enough. You need to reward those who follow your lead, so others see the benefit of staying in line. The carrot makes them *want* to obey; the stick makes sure they *have to*.

The most effective kind of fear isn't loud or violent—it's a shadow that follows them everywhere. They don't have to see you coming to know you're there. They don't have to hear the threat to understand the danger. That's when you've won. That's when obedience becomes instinct.

Bottom line? Fear isn't about screaming and threats. It's about making people so uncertain, so paranoid about what might happen, that they never even think about challenging you. And once you have them in that state, you own them.

Tactic 17.3:
Silent Authority: The Power of Saying Nothing

Weak men run their mouths. Real power doesn't come from loud threats, constant explanations, or desperate attempts to prove dominance. It comes from **silence**—controlled, intentional, and suffocating. The most feared people in any room aren't the ones barking orders. They're the ones who say the least, making everyone wonder what the fuck they're thinking.

Silence makes people uneasy. It forces them to fill in the blanks with their own paranoia. When you hold back, they scramble to interpret your thoughts, trying to predict your reaction, trying to stay on your good side—even when you haven't said a damn thing. That's control. That's power. And the best part? You never even had to lift a fucking finger.

Here's how to weaponize silence and make people dance without saying a word:

- **Pause Before You Speak:** Don't rush to answer a question, agree to a deal, or react to bullshit. Let silence stretch. Watch them get nervous, over-explain, or backpedal before you even respond. Most people talk themselves into a weaker position if you just let them.

- **Never Explain Yourself:** The second you start explaining, you've already lost. Strong people don't justify their decisions. They make them, and people adjust. "Because I said so" isn't just for parents—it's for anyone who understands that power doesn't beg to be understood.

- **Respond With a Look, Not Words:** Someone disrespects you? Don't react. Just stare at them. Make them sweat. Let the weight of your silence crush their confidence. A well-timed pause can make even the biggest asshole start doubting himself.

- **Make Others Talk First:** The one who speaks first in a negotiation usually loses. Hold your ground. Let them fidget, stumble, and blurt out their real concerns before you ever open your mouth. They'll reveal everything if you let them.

- **Disappear When Necessary:** When people don't have constant access to you, they value your time more. They start wondering what you're thinking, if they've pissed you off, or if they're being left behind. A little absence creates dependence.

Silence isn't weakness—it's control. It makes people desperate for your approval, anxious for your response, and scared to step out of line. When you stop talking, people start thinking. And when they start thinking, they start *fearing*. That's when you know you own them.

Bottom line? Power doesn't need to announce itself. It doesn't need to yell, argue, or explain. The less you say, the more they scramble to understand you. And that's when you know you've already won.

Tactic 17.4:
Death by Doubt: Planting Seeds That Destroy Trust

Power isn't about being the strongest—it's about making sure your enemies are too weak to fight back. The fastest way to dismantle any organization, partnership, or alliance isn't with an open attack. It's with **doubt**. Once people start questioning each other, their loyalty, their motives, and their competence, it's only a matter of time before everything collapses under the weight of its own paranoia.

Trust is the foundation of power structures. Destroy that, and everything else follows. You don't need proof. You don't need direct confrontation. You just need to plant the right **seeds of doubt** and let human nature do the rest. Once doubt takes hold, it spreads like a virus, infecting every interaction, turning allies into enemies, and making even the most confident leader second-guess their own shadow.

Here's how to inject poison into any group without ever getting caught:

- **Be the Subtle Observer:** People lower their guard around someone who listens more than they talk. Position yourself as the person who "notices things" but doesn't stir the pot—at least, not directly. Make people *come to you* for information instead of pushing it on them.

- **Use Questions, Not Accusations:** A well-placed question is more dangerous than a direct attack. "Did you notice how they've been acting different lately?" "Do you think they're looking out for your best interest?" You're not telling them anything—you're **making them tell themselves**.

- **Let Them Do the Work:** Give just enough information for them to start doubting, then step back and let their paranoia fill in the blanks. People will always believe their own suspicions over an outright lie, so **nudge them, but let them build the conspiracy themselves**.

- **Make Mistrust Public:** Encourage casual "off-the-record" conversations in group settings. **"I probably shouldn't say anything, but..."** works like a charm. Once someone repeats what you planted, it stops being *your* idea—it becomes *theirs*.

- **Trigger Overreactions:** Once the cracks appear, push people into defensive positions. A small, well-timed comment can make them lash out, exposing their own insecurity. Suddenly, they're the ones proving they're untrustworthy—not you.

By the time they realize what's happened, their entire support system will be in ruins. No one will trust anyone. Every word will be second-guessed. Every action will be scrutinized. And you? You'll be standing on the sidelines, **watching them destroy themselves**.

Bottom line? Trust is fragile. A whisper can do more damage than a scream. If you know how to make people question everything, you never have to lift a finger—**they'll take each other out for you**.

Tactic 17.5:
The Implosion Blueprint: Letting Them Destroy Themselves

The most efficient way to take down a rival isn't with an attack —it's by making sure they **self-destruct**. The smartest predators don't waste energy chasing their prey; they let it **run itself to death**. That's what this is about—**orchestrating collapse without leaving your fingerprints on the wreckage**.

People, businesses, and organizations fail for the same reasons —**infighting, bad decisions, and uncontrolled chaos**. You don't need to push them over the edge. You just need to remove the guardrails, let them pick up speed, and watch them **drive straight into a wall**.

Here's how to set the stage for their downfall:

- **Feed Their Worst Instincts:** Everyone has weaknesses—**arrogance, greed, impulsiveness, paranoia**. Nudge them toward the behaviors that will **sink them faster**. Stroke an egomaniac's ego until they overreach. Encourage a control freak's paranoia until they alienate their allies. Let their **own flaws do the damage**.

- **Overload Them with Distractions:** If they're too busy putting out fires, they won't see the real danger coming. Stir up pointless conflicts, flood them with misinformation, **keep them spinning in circles** until exhaustion takes over.

- **Accelerate Their Failures:** When they start making mistakes, **don't intervene**. Let them double down on bad decisions. If a strategy is failing, **convince them it just needs more time, more money, more effort**. The deeper they sink, the harder it is to climb out.

- **Turn Their Allies Against Them:** When things go south, people look for someone to blame. Make sure **all fingers point at them**. Feed their allies just enough doubt to **start questioning their leadership, their judgment, their motives**. Once loyalty cracks, collapse is inevitable.

- **Make Escape Impossible:** Give them just enough hope to keep them from bailing early. If they know they're doomed, they'll cut their losses and move on. But if they believe they can turn it around, they'll stay in the fight long enough to **lose everything**.

By the time they realize what's happening, **it's too late**. Their credibility is shattered. Their supporters have abandoned them. Their resources are drained. And the best part? They'll be too busy blaming themselves, each other, or **some imaginary enemy** to ever see the real mastermind behind it all.

Bottom line? The most **brutal** takedown is the one that looks like **an accident**. Let them think they're in control, let them sabotage themselves, and when the dust settles—**you'll be the only one left standing**.

> *Control doesn't come from chaos—it comes from owning the rhythm of destruction. When you make people fear calm more than conflict, you've already beaten them. Manipulation, fear, silence, and doubt aren't tactics—they're instruments. Play them long enough, and even the strong start dancing to your tune.*

Lesson 18: Psychological Defense–Becoming Untouchable

Tactic 18.1:
The Power of Indifference: Why Not Giving a Shit Is a
Superpower

The person who cares less **always** wins. That's not philosophy —it's psychological fact. The second you show **attachment, desperation, or emotional investment**, you hand over control. The second they see you **need** something, they have leverage. The antidote? **Indifference.** The ability to walk away from anything, anyone, or any situation without hesitation.

Most people are weak because they **fear loss**—loss of approval, status, relationships, money. They cling, they beg, they **bend** just to keep things from slipping through their fingers. That's why they're **easy to manipulate**. A man who's afraid to lose something can be controlled. A man who **doesn't give a fuck** about losing can't be controlled. He sets the terms.

Here's how to weaponize indifference and make people chase **you** instead of the other way around:

- **Silence = Power:** When someone pushes you for an answer, make them wait. That discomfort they feel? That's you owning the situation. Indifference makes them **want** your approval, your time, your decision.

- **Never Show Desperation:** The more someone **needs** something, the less valuable it becomes. If they think you'll fold under pressure, they'll press harder. But if they sense you'll **walk away without hesitation**, they'll scramble to keep you.

- **Make Them Prove Themselves to You:** When you act like you don't need someone, they start **needing** you.

Reverse the dynamic. Instead of **chasing**, make them **earn** your time, your trust, your cooperation.

- ◉ **Be Willing to Burn the Bridge:** Nothing terrifies manipulators more than someone who doesn't fear **cutting them off**. The ability to say "Fuck this" and **walk away mid-game** makes them desperate to regain control. Let them sweat.

- ◉ **Control Your Reactions:** People test you to see what buttons they can push. If you react emotionally, they **own you**. But if you stay calm, unreadable, and detached? **They lose power, and you gain it.**

Indifference isn't about **laziness**. It's about **control**. It makes people chase you, respect you, and **fear losing you**—whether it's in business, relationships, or negotiations. The moment they think they have you on a leash, **cut the fucking rope** and watch them panic.

Bottom line? The one who cares less **always wins**. The second you become comfortable with walking away from anything, **you become the one in control**—because they'll be the ones afraid to lose *you*.

Tactic 18.2:
Preemptive Strikes: Hit First, Ask Questions Never

In the game of power, **waiting to be attacked is a fucking death sentence**. The people who hesitate, who "wait and see," who try to play defense? They get steamrolled. You don't win by responding. You win by **moving first, hitting hard, and making damn sure they never recover**. That's the power of the **preemptive strike**—neutralizing threats before they even become a problem.

Most people are too soft for this. They wait until the threat is obvious, until the damage is already happening. But by the time you're **reacting**, you've already lost **control**. The real players don't wait. They **identify threats early, hit first, and leave nothing standing**. If you see an enemy forming, **eliminate them before they ever get a chance to step up**.

Here's how to execute the **perfect preemptive strike**:

- **Spot the Threats Early:** Your biggest mistake is thinking problems **suddenly appear**. They don't. Every betrayal, every attack, every downfall was **building for a while**. Stay paranoid. Watch for shifts in loyalty, whispers of competition, signs of an enemy getting stronger.

- **Strike Before They Expect It:** The best attack is the one they **never** see coming. If someone's gathering influence, **undermine them quietly**. If a rival business is gaining traction, **cut off their resources** before they even realize you're watching. If someone is plotting against you, **destroy their credibility before they make a move**.

- **Leave No Room for Comebacks:** Half-measures get you killed. If you're going to take someone out, **do it completely**. Ruin their alliances, damage their reputation, ensure they have **no path back to power**. Make them so weak they **don't even think about revenge**.

- **Use Fear as a Deterrent:** If people know you **strike first**, they'll be too scared to challenge you. Make an example out of someone early, and the rest will **fall in line** without you having to lift a finger.

- **Keep Your Hands Clean:** A preemptive strike shouldn't look like an attack—it should look like a **natural collapse**. The best power moves happen in the shadows. Let them **think they destroyed themselves** while you **stand there untouched**.

The world isn't kind to the **hesitant**. The ones who wait to be attacked **never last**. If you want to survive, you don't wait for threats to grow—you **cut them off at the fucking root**.

Bottom line? If you think someone might be a problem, they already are. Strike first, strike hard, and make damn sure they never get the chance to hit back. **Hesitation is a luxury for the weak. Move first, or die waiting.**

Tactic18.3:
The Predator's Mindset: Never Think Like Prey

Survival isn't about being the **strongest**—it's about being the one who **refuses to be hunted**. The world is divided into two kinds of people: **predators and prey**. Prey waits for permission, follows the rules, and **hopes for fairness**. Predators **take what they want, dictate the rules, and never ask for shit**. If you're not thinking like a predator, you're just waiting to be someone else's next meal.

Most people get manipulated, controlled, or crushed because they **think like prey**. They want to be liked, they want approval, they believe that if they just "do the right thing," everything will work out. **It won't.** The world isn't fair. The game is rigged. And the only ones who survive are the ones who **know how to play dirty when they need to**.

Here's how to develop the **predator's mindset** and make sure you're the one in control:

- ⦿ **Kill the Need for Validation:** Prey seek approval. They need reassurance, permission, someone to tell them they're doing fine. **Predators don't give a shit.** They make their own decisions and let everyone else adjust.

The less you care about being liked, the harder you are to control.

- **Always Be on Offense:** Prey react. Predators **anticipate**. You don't wait for problems to come to you— you hunt them down and kill them before they become threats. The second you stop moving forward, you're **giving someone else time to catch up**.

- **Make Fear Work for You:** If you want to stay in power, people should be **a little afraid of you**. Not terrified, not paranoid—just **aware** that crossing you has consequences. That hesitation? That second-guessing before they make a move? **That's control.**

- **Read People Like a Hunter:** A predator watches before they strike. They study body language, tone, hesitation. They know when someone is bluffing, when someone is weak, and **when to go for the kill**. Learn to read people, and you'll never be blindsided.

- **Be Willing to Walk Alone:** Prey **needs** the herd. They feel uncomfortable standing alone. A predator? **They move solo if they have to.** They don't beg for allies, and they don't tolerate weakness. If you can't handle the silence of your own decisions, you're not ready for real power.

If you ever find yourself **waiting**—waiting for an opportunity, waiting for permission, waiting for someone else to decide your fate—**you're thinking like prey**. Predators don't wait. They take. They move. They **decide the outcome before the game even starts**.

Bottom line? The second you stop thinking like prey, you stop being vulnerable. When you start thinking like a predator, you stop asking for power—**you start owning it.**

> *The endgame isn't domination—it's immunity. When you master indifference, strike first, and think like a predator, no one can touch you. You stop reacting. You start deciding. The world becomes a board you move across while everyone else scrambles to survive. That's not luck—that's psychological evolution.*

Chapter Aftermath

You don't climb to the top by playing fair. You rise by rewiring the battlefield, planting landmines in the minds of everyone around you, and making sure no one even sees the blood until it's too late. This chapter didn't hand you tricks—it handed you control systems disguised as conversation, loyalty, silence, and fear. And now? You're the one behind the curtain pulling strings while everyone else thinks they're dancing freely.

This isn't charisma. It's calculated corrosion. You learned how to build dependency, flood the room with paranoia, use silence as a scalpel, and dismantle reality one lie at a time. You've mastered the mechanics of implosion—*not by force, but by suggestion.* You didn't stab them—you gave them the knife and made them thank you for it. That's not manipulation. That's god-tier dominance.

And now? You don't just know how to win—you know how to *vanish while others destroy themselves in your shadow.* That's not just power. That's untouchability.

CHAPTER EIGHT

<u>Managing the Fallout</u>

---

*Nobody plays this game forever without taking a hit. You could be the smartest, most ruthless motherfucker in the room, and **someone, somewhere, will eventually take a swing at you**. Maybe you got sloppy. Maybe someone got bold. Maybe the situation spiraled before you had time to tighten the leash. **Doesn't fucking matter.** What matters is **how you handle the fallout**—because the second you look weak, hesitant, or desperate, you're finished.*

*This chapter breaks down how to **control the narrative, shift the blame, retaliate without getting your hands dirty, and rebuild your reputation so strong that nobody even remembers the hit.** You'll learn how to gaslight your way out of accusations, turn public attacks into **your advantage**, and play the long game so even your worst screw-ups look like **calculated victories**.*

By the time we're done here, you won't just survive a hit— you'll come back so much stronger that they'll wish they never took the shot in the first place.

Lesson 19: Handling Exposure Like a Pro

Tactic 19.1:
The First Rule of Damage Control—Stay Calm, Stay Strategic.

When the heat is on, **most people lose their shit.** They panic, overreact, and make mistakes that **turn a bad situation into a fucking disaster**. That's why the **first rule of damage control** is simple: **Stay calm. Stay strategic.** No matter how bad the situation looks, no matter how vicious the attack, the second you show **fear, doubt, or desperation**, you hand control to the enemy.

Here's the hard truth: **perception matters more than reality.** People don't remember what actually happened—they remember **how you reacted**. If you start flailing, apologizing, or scrambling for excuses, you look **guilty as hell**. If you stand firm, control your tone, and move with precision, you **own the situation**.

Here's how to **lock down your response and take control before the narrative gets away from you**:

- **Control Your Immediate Reaction:** The first move after an attack is the most critical. **DO NOT react emotionally.** Don't respond out of anger. Don't jump to defend yourself. Don't start explaining shit. **Pause. Process. Plan.** The person who moves first in a panic always loses.

- **Gather Intel Before Making a Move:** Before you say **a single fucking word**, assess the situation. What do people actually know? What proof exists? Who's behind this? What's their angle? **You don't fight an enemy blind—you gather intelligence and strike when you're ready.**

- **Limit Public Statements:** The more you talk, the more ammo you give your enemies. **Silence makes people nervous.** When they don't know what you're thinking, they start guessing. And when they guess, they **make mistakes.** Let them overplay their hand before you even step in.

- **Set the Right Tone:** When you do respond, you need to come across as **unshaken and in control.** Short, confident, no rambling, no excuses. **Example:** "I'm aware of the situation, and I'm handling it." That one sentence is more powerful than a 10-page speech.

- **Never Act Like You're on the Defensive:** The moment you **defend,** you look weak. Instead of proving your innocence, shift the burden. **Example:** "People love to spread misinformation. I don't waste my time on rumors." Now they're the ones who look desperate for pushing the issue.

**The key to surviving any attack is controlling the damage—
not letting the damage control you. The second you start **scrambling, explaining, or begging for understanding, you're dead in the water. You move with strategy, you act when the time is right, and you **make sure the next move is yours—not theirs.**

Bottom line? Panic is the enemy. Hesitation is death. Stay calm, stay in control, and by the time they realize you're still standing, they'll be the ones falling apart.

Tactic 19.2:
Weaponizing Sympathy—How to Turn the Attack on Them

When someone comes for you, they expect **pushback, denial, maybe even a counterattack.** What they don't expect is for **you to flip the script so hard that they end up looking like the**

asshole while you walk away with public sympathy. That's the power of **weaponized sympathy**—turning yourself into the victim so effectively that **they** are the ones who get scrutinized, doubted, and ultimately burned.

People are **emotional idiots.** They don't care about facts—they care about **how they feel about a situation.** If you make them **feel** like you've been wronged, logic takes a backseat. You don't have to prove innocence—you just have to make the attacker look like they're **bullying, exaggerating, or being unfair.**

Here's how to take their attack and turn it into **your advantage**:

- ⊙ **Act Deeply "Hurt" by the Accusation:** People expect defensiveness. **Instead, look wounded.** Shake your head, exhale slowly, maybe even laugh in disbelief. "Wow. I never thought I'd hear something like that from *you*." Make them feel like **they** just betrayed *you*, not the other way around.

- ⊙ **Subtly Position Yourself as the Real Victim:** "I get that people are looking for someone to blame, but this? *This* is low." Now you've established that the accuser is **lashing out unfairly**, rather than exposing any real wrongdoing.

- ⊙ **Play the "Misunderstood" Card:** "If you really knew me, you'd know I'd never do something like that." This forces them to either **double down (and look like an asshole) or hesitate (and lose credibility).** Either way, you just shifted the power dynamic.

- ⊙ **Turn Their Own Tactics Against Them:** If they're trying to use emotion, **out-emotion them.** If they're acting outraged, look *heartbroken*. If they're trying to stay calm, throw in a little raw disappointment: "I expected better from you." That line alone can make **anyone hesitate.**

- **Force Others to Defend You:** "I'm not even going to argue. People who know me will know the truth." Now, you've just made everyone around you feel **obligated to take your side**—because who the fuck wants to be seen siding with a bully?

People don't **care** about facts. They care about **who looks like the bigger asshole.** The moment you make **them** look aggressive, overreaching, or cruel, the whole game **flips in your favor.**

Bottom line? The best way to kill an accusation isn't to deny it —it's to make the attacker look like the **real villain.** Once they're the one on the defensive, **you don't even need to prove shit.**

Tactic 19.3:
Destroying Their Credibility Without Leaving Fingerprints

Discrediting someone isn't about **proving them wrong**—it's about **making sure no one listens to them in the first place.** If they lose credibility, it doesn't matter what they say, how loud they scream, or how much evidence they think they have—**no one will take them seriously.** That's the game. You don't argue. You don't debate. You just **make them look unreliable, unstable, or self-serving** until their voice is nothing more than background noise.

The key is to do it **without looking like you're behind it.** If people see you actively tearing someone down, you risk looking defensive or malicious. But if you make it look **like they destroyed themselves?** That's when the magic happens.

Here's how to **erase someone's credibility without leaving a trace**:

- **Let Them Overplay Their Hand:** People who want to take you down always go **too far.** They exaggerate, they embellish, they push too hard. Let them dig their own grave, then casually highlight their inconsistencies: *"Wait… last week they said it was X. Now it's Y? Interesting."* That's all it takes to plant doubt.

- **Spread "Concerns" Instead of Accusations:** Never outright call them a liar—that makes it a fight. Instead, **raise gentle concerns** that make people doubt them. *"I've heard they have a habit of twisting things to fit their narrative, but hey, who knows?"* You didn't accuse them of shit, but now everyone is questioning them.

- **Highlight Their Motivations:** If people think the accuser has an **agenda**, their words become worthless. "Kinda weird they're making all this noise right after getting passed up for that promotion, huh?" Now everything they say **looks like a personal grudge, not the truth.**

- **Use the "They're Unstable" Card:** If they seem emotional, **use it against them**. "They've been really stressed lately… hope they're doing okay." If they *don't* seem emotional, **push the idea that they're cold and calculating**. "They always know just the right time to stir up drama, huh?" Either way, **you frame them as manipulative.**

- **Encourage Their Self-Destruction:** Give them **just enough rope** to hang themselves. Feed their anger, let them rant, **make sure more people hear them acting irrational.** The crazier they look, the easier it is to dismiss them.

The best credibility assassinations **don't look like assassinations.** You're not attacking them. You're not even fighting back. **You're just subtly guiding public perception until no one believes a word they say.**

Bottom line? If they can't be trusted, they can't hurt you. **Make their own words work against them, and by the time they realize what's happening, no one will be listening anymore.**

> *Crisis doesn't reveal character—it reveals control. Panic exposes amateurs, silence crowns professionals. The ones who survive aren't innocent; they're disciplined. They keep their mouths shut, their faces calm, and their knives clean. You don't outrun exposure—you outlast it.*

Lesson 20: Retaliating Without Getting Caught

Tactic 20.1:
The Silent Rebuild—How to Regain Control After a Setback

When you take a hit, **your first instinct might be to come out swinging, clear your name, and prove your enemies wrong. Wrong move.** That's what they expect. That's what they're *hoping* you'll do—react emotionally, overcorrect, and expose yourself to even more attacks. **The real power move? You go silent, regroup, and rebuild from the shadows.**

The **Silent Rebuild** is about **regaining control without making noise**. It's about **strengthening your position while they still think you're down.** When done right, by the time they realize you've recovered, you'll already be **five steps ahead and untouchable**.

Here's how you **rebuild power without showing your hand**:

- **Step 1: Go Dark, Go Quiet**

  The more you talk after a hit, the more mistakes you make. **Silence forces them to fill in the blanks with their own paranoia.** Disappear from the conversation, keep your moves private, and **make them wonder what you're planning.**

- **Step 2: Lock Down Your Core Alliances**

  After a hit, some people will distance themselves. **Let them go.** They were weak. Focus on the people who stick around—**reinforce their loyalty**. Make it clear that sticking with you is in their best interest.

- **Step 3: Gather Intelligence While They're Distracted**

  While they're celebrating your downfall, **you're studying them.** Who's talking the most? Who's benefiting from your setback? **Find out who really pulled the strings**— because when the time comes, they're the ones who need to be dealt with first.

- **Step 4: Rebuild Your Power, Piece by Piece**

  Instead of a big, public comeback, **reconstruct your position quietly.** Strengthen your connections, cut off weaknesses, **build leverage while they think you're still recovering.** When they finally see you've rebuilt, it'll be **too late to stop you.**

- **Step 5: Return With Precision, Not Emotion**

  When you make your move, **don't do it out of anger— do it out of strategy.** Whether it's reclaiming lost ground, crushing the people who tried to bury you, or flipping the entire situation in your favor, **make sure your return is undeniable.**

People **love** a downfall story. They love thinking they've won. **Use that.** Let them lower their guard, let them write you off. By the time they realize you were never out of the game, **you'll already be running it again.**

Bottom line? When you take a hit, you don't **panic**—you **disappear, regroup, and return stronger than ever.** And when you do? **Make sure they never get another chance to hit you again.**

Tactic 20.2:
The "Fake Apology" Trick—Saying Sorry Without Admitting Guilt

Most people **fuck themselves over** the moment they apologize. They think saying "sorry" will make things go away. **Wrong.** A real apology is an admission of guilt, a surrender, a confirmation that you fucked up. **And once you give them that? They own you.**

But here's the thing—sometimes, you have to **play the game**. Sometimes, public perception forces your hand, and people expect an apology. That's when you use **the Fake Apology Trick**—you say just enough to calm the storm, without actually admitting to a damn thing. **You give them the illusion of regret while keeping control of the narrative.**

Here's how you **apologize without taking the fall**:

- ◉ **Make It About Their Feelings, Not Your Actions**
  A real apology takes responsibility. **A fake apology shifts focus.** Instead of saying, *"I was wrong,"* say, *"I'm sorry you feel that way."* It acknowledges emotions **without admitting fault.**

◉ **Use Vague, Non-Committal Language**

The more specific an apology, the more they can use it against you. Keep it **broad and empty**:

- *"Mistakes were made."* (Not *who* made them.)

- *"I could have handled things differently."* (No specifics, no real admission.)

- *"I regret how this situation unfolded."* (Sounds like remorse, **but says nothing.**)

◉ **Shift the Blame Subtly**

Never fully own the problem. Instead, sprinkle in context that **shares the responsibility**:

- *"I see now that there was a misunderstanding."* (*Translation: It's not my fault you misinterpreted.*)

- *"I wish communication had been clearer."* (*Translation: Other people contributed to this mess.*)

◉ **Close with a Power Move, Not Submission**

End the apology by re-establishing control:

- *"I'm moving forward with lessons learned."* (**You control the outcome.**)

- *"I hope we can all take something from this."* (**Now it's *their* problem too.**)

- *"I appreciate those who continue to support me."* (**Creates an 'us vs. them' dynamic.**)

People don't actually care about apologies—they care about **who wins the perception battle.** A good fake apology **shuts down drama without weakening your position.** By the time they realize you never actually admitted to anything, **the storm has already passed.**

Bottom line? Never give them **a real apology to use against you.** Say just enough to keep the peace, keep your hands clean, and **walk away with your power intact.**

Tactic 20.3:
The Blame Shift Game—How to Make Someone Else the Fall Guy

When shit goes south, **someone has to take the fall**—and it sure as hell shouldn't be you. The difference between **losers and survivors** is simple: **losers take the hit, survivors redirect it.** That's the game. When you're caught in a mess, **you don't defend yourself—you shift the weight onto someone else.**

Blame is a currency. If you know how to **transfer it, dilute it, or redirect it**, you walk away **clean** while someone else is left explaining themselves. Most people are **too slow, too honest, or too naive** to understand this. But not you. By the time they realize what happened, **they're too busy saving their own ass to come after yours.**

Here's how you master **The Blame Shift Game** and make sure you're never the one left holding the bag:

- ◉ **Step 1: Introduce Doubt Immediately**

  The longer blame sits on you, **the harder it is to shake off.** Before accusations even take hold, start **casting shadows in other directions.**

  - *"I wasn't the only one involved in that decision."*

  - *"That's not how I remember it. We should double-check who was responsible."*

- *"I thought that was handled by someone else."*
Your goal isn't to **point fingers just yet**—it's to make people pause before they lock in on you.

◉ **Step 2: Redirect the Narrative Subtly**

Instead of **denying involvement**, shift the focus to **someone else's role in the situation.**

- *"From what I understand, this started before I was even involved."*

- *"I was just following the information I was given."*

- *"I assumed the right steps had already been taken by management."*
Notice how none of these statements are outright accusations. **They just make people start asking different questions.**

◉ **Step 3: Play the "Miscommunication" Card**

Most screw-ups happen because **someone dropped the ball.** If you frame the situation as a **miscommunication**, you create **doubt without looking like you're attacking anyone.**

- *"I was under the impression that things were on track."*

- *"I was told this was already handled, so I didn't interfere."*

- *"I didn't have all the information at the time."*
These statements **buy you time** and force people to dig deeper **instead of immediately blaming you.**

◉ **Step 4: Let Them Fight Each Other**

If there's a group involved, your best move is to **subtly pit them against each other** so they forget about you entirely.

- *"I just assumed Jake and Sarah were handling it."*

- *"I wasn't in those meetings, so I'm not sure who made that final call."*

- *"I remember someone mentioning a different approach, but I don't know who pushed for it."*
  Now they're too busy **arguing over whose fault it really is**, and you? **You're already walking away from the explosion.**

◉ **Step 5: Reinforce Your Innocence Last**

Once the dust settles and someone else is under fire, **you step in like the voice of reason.**

- *"I never meant for this to be such a big issue."*

- *"If I had known earlier, I would have stepped in to help."*

- *"Hopefully we all learn from this and communicate better next time."*
  Now, instead of being blamed, you look like the only reasonable person left in the room.

Now, here's the **real game-changer**—you don't just **escape blame.** You come out of this **stronger than before.** By the time the smoke clears, people **trust you more**, not less. Why? Because you weren't fighting to prove your innocence—you were "helping clarify the situation." **You didn't dodge the bullet; you made them hand you the fucking gun.**

Bottom line? When blame starts flying, don't sit there like a target. **Redirect it, confuse it, and by the time they realize what happened, they'll be too busy fighting each other to even remember your name.** The best escape is **one where you walk away not just untouched—but respected.**

Revenge isn't rage—it's architecture. You rebuild while they gloat, smile while they burn, and strike only when the timing makes silence look suspicious. The loud ones swing fists; the smart ones write blueprints for collapse. Retaliation done right doesn't echo—it erases.

Lesson 21: Controlling the Perception War

Tactic 21.1
Why Silence Can Be the Most Powerful Response

When people get attacked, most of them **can't shut the fuck up.** They scramble to explain themselves, deny accusations, or "clear the air." **Big mistake.** The more you talk, the more ammo you give your enemies. The more you explain, the guiltier you look. **Silence, on the other hand, is terrifying.** It makes people nervous, it makes them doubt their own attack, and most importantly—it forces them to **fill in the blanks.**

Silence isn't inaction. **It's a weapon.** Used correctly, it makes you look **untouchable, unbothered, and more powerful than any loudmouth trying to drag you into the mud.** People fear what they **don't understand**, and nothing is harder to read than someone who **refuses to engage.**

Here's how to make **silence your strongest play**:

- ⊙ **Let Them Talk Themselves Into a Corner**
  When someone comes after you, they expect you to **respond immediately**. When you don't, they **panic.**

- They'll **escalate** their attacks, pushing harder for a reaction.

- They'll start **contradicting themselves**, trying to prove their point.

- They'll look **desperate and obsessed** while you stay cool and detached.
  By the time you do speak—**if you even need to**—they've already **burned their own credibility.**

◉ **Create Psychological Pressure by Leaving a Void**

Silence **makes people uncomfortable**. It forces them to **fill in the gaps themselves**, and their imagination will do more damage than you ever could.

- *"Why aren't they responding? Do they know something I don't?"*

- *"Are they planning something?"*

- *"Did I just make a mistake?"*
  The moment they start second-guessing themselves, you win.

◉ **Make Your Absence More Powerful Than Their Presence**

Some battles aren't worth fighting. **Sometimes, the best move is to disappear.** If you remove yourself from the conversation, you instantly become **bigger than the drama.**

- If people keep **talking about you after you've gone quiet**, you've already **won.**

- If your silence **makes others start defending you**, they're now fighting your battle for you.

- If they move on because they got nothing from you, then **the attack failed.** Either way, **you didn't lose shit.**

⦿ **Break the Pattern by Speaking on Your Terms**

Silence works best when it's **intentional.** If you do respond, **make it count.**

- Wait until **they're tired, sloppy, or exposed.**

- Respond with **a single, controlled statement**— something cold and dismissive, like:

   ✓ *"Not worth my time."*

   ✓ *"People believe what they want."*

   ✓ *"I don't explain myself to nobodies."*

That one **short response** will have **more impact than a thousand explanations.**

Here's the real kicker—**silence makes people project their own fears onto you.** They assume you're **calm because you know something they don't.** They assume you're **planning something bigger.** They assume **they fucked up.**

Bottom line? When you go silent, you don't just control the conversation—you control their mind. Let them wonder. Let them panic. Let them **talk themselves into defeat while you stay untouchable.**

Tactic 21.2:
The Art of the Slow Narrative Shift—Turning an Enemy Into a Fool Over Time

Winning a fight isn't always about **immediate destruction.** Sometimes, the best strategy is **patience**—letting your enemy **bury themselves** while you slowly turn the story against them. A direct attack can be risky, but a **slow, controlled narrative shift?** That's a long game they won't even realize they're losing until it's too late.

The trick isn't to prove them wrong right away. **That's what they expect.** Instead, you let them **run their mouth, overplay their hand, and exhaust their credibility**, while you **methodically chip away at their position, little by little, until they look like a complete fool.**

Here's how you do it:

- ◉ **Let Them Set the Bar Too High**
  When someone launches an attack, they often go **too far, making big claims they can't fully support.** You don't need to refute them immediately—**just let them keep talking.**

  - The more extreme their accusations, the more likely they'll **say something stupid.**

  - If they claim to have evidence, let them **dig their own hole trying to produce it.**

  - If they act like they know everything, wait until they **contradict themselves.**
    Over time, their credibility erodes **without you even lifting a finger.**

  - **Quietly Undermine the Foundation of Their Story**
    Instead of going head-to-head, you **attack their argument from the sides.**

  - If they're pushing a narrative, **ask innocent questions that expose the cracks.**

    ✓ *"Interesting. Where exactly did you hear that?"*

    ✓ *"Huh, I thought the details were different."*

    ✓ *"Strange, that's not what I've been told."*

- If they're using emotional manipulation, **stay calm and let them escalate.** Their overreaction will make them look **unstable.**

- If they're painting themselves as the hero, **introduce doubt subtly.** "It's odd how they always seem to be at the center of drama."

- **Reframe the Narrative Without Directly Attacking** Once doubt has set in, you **slowly reposition yourself as the reasonable one.**

- Instead of saying *they're lying*, frame them as **misguided, misinformed, or emotional.**

  ✓ *"I don't think they're doing this maliciously... they just don't have all the facts."*

  ✓ *"I'm sure they believe what they're saying, even if it's not completely accurate."*

- The moment people start **questioning their credibility,** their entire attack **loses weight.**

◉ **Let Time Do the Work**
A slow narrative shift is about **making people lose interest in the drama** until your enemy is just **a clown shouting into the void.**

- Their words stop carrying weight because **they've cried wolf too many times.**

- People begin **rolling their eyes** when their name comes up.

- Eventually, **they destroy their own credibility**—and you never had to throw a direct punch. **Bottom line?** A quick attack is obvious. **A slow, controlled shift in perception is unstoppable.** Let them **talk**

themselves into looking like a fool, while you sit back, **pulling the strings and rewriting the story one subtle move at a time.**

Bottom line? A quick attack is obvious. **A slow, controlled shift in perception is unstoppable.** Let them **talk themselves into looking like a fool**, while you sit back, **pulling the strings and rewriting the story one subtle move at a time.** And the best part? **By the time they realize they've lost, they won't even remember who led them there.**

Tactic 21.3:
How to Rebuild Your Image After a Public Hit

When your reputation takes a hit, **most people panic and try to fix it overnight. Wrong move.** A reputation isn't rebuilt with a **grand statement or a desperate PR stunt**—it's rebuilt **strategically, over time**, without looking like you're trying too hard. If you overcorrect, you look guilty. If you react emotionally, you look weak. **The only way to win is through controlled, calculated moves that make people forget you ever took the hit in the first place.**

People have **short memories**, but only if you play this right. The key is to **rebuild without looking like you're scrambling to recover. If you do this right, you won't just fix your image— you'll come out looking even stronger than before.**

Here's how you take back control:

- ◉ **Step 1: Let the Dust Settle Before You Move**

  - The worst thing you can do after a hit is **react too fast.** The moment you try to defend yourself or change the narrative immediately, **you look like you're covering your ass.**

- Instead, **go quiet.** Give people time to **move on to the next scandal, the next drama.**

- If people don't see you **scrambling to fix the damage,** they won't assume it was that bad.

◉ **Step 2: Subtly Reinforce Your Value**

- Once the heat dies down, start **making quiet moves to remind people why you were respected in the first place.**

- No public statements, no apologies—just **deliver results.**

- If you're in business, **close a big deal.** If you're in leadership, **make a smart, decisive move.** If you're in social circles, **let your connections work for you.**

◉ **Step 3: Control the Narrative Through Association**

- People remember **who you stand next to.** If your name is tied to **successful, respected figures,** your reputation naturally rebounds.

- Start aligning with **credible, powerful people.**

- A single photo, a casual endorsement, or a mutual connection can **wipe out weeks of negative press.**

◉ **Step 4: Let Time Erase the Damage**

- Time is your greatest weapon. **Most scandals die out in weeks, sometimes days.**

- **Stop feeding the fire.** The more you try to "prove" you've recovered, the longer people will **associate you with the damage.**

- If you let time do the work, **your name will outlast the scandal.**

Now here's the real move—**you don't just recover.** You **come back stronger.** You **use the hit as proof** that you can take damage and keep moving. **People respect resilience more than perfection.** And by the time you're done, **no one will remember the fall—they'll only remember the comeback.**

Bottom line? A ruined reputation isn't permanent—unless you act like it is. Stay calm, play the long game, and let **your results, your alliances, and time itself** do the work for you. By the time people realize you've recovered, **you'll already be ten steps ahead.**

Tactic 21.4:
Turning Your Setbacks into Power Moves

People love **comeback stories, but only if they're framed the right way.** If you handle it wrong, your past mistakes will **follow you forever.** But if you play this right, **your biggest failures can be turned into reasons people respect you even more.**

The trick? **You don't just survive past mistakes—you turn them into evidence that you're stronger, smarter, and more dangerous than before.**

Here's how to **convert failure into power:**

- ◉ **Step 1: Own the Story Before Someone Else Does**

    - If you let people **define your failures**, you'll always be on the defensive. Instead, **control the narrative yourself.**

    - How? **You bring it up first**—but on your own terms.

        ✓ *"That moment was brutal, but I needed it."*

    ✓ *"Honestly, I'd be nowhere near as sharp today if I hadn't gone through that."*

    ✓ *"That was the moment I learned how the game really works."*

- Now, instead of them **using it against you**, they see it as **a lesson that made you better.**

◉ **Step 2: Reframe the Setback as a Strength**

- You don't just admit to past failures—you **show how they turned you into a stronger version of yourself.**

- The key here is **positioning:**

    ✓ *If you got screwed over? → "That's when I learned how to spot snakes."*

    ✓ *If you took a big loss? → "That experience taught me how to rebuild from nothing."*

    ✓ *If you made a mistake? → "That's when I realized what real power looks like."*

- Every setback becomes **part of your power arc.**

◉ **Step 3: Make It Look Like You Passed a Test Others Wouldn't Survive**

- **People respect survivors.** If you position yourself as someone who **took damage but came out smarter, meaner, and sharper**, you gain authority.

- The trick is to make sure the story **reinforces your credibility.**

    ✓ *"Most people wouldn't have bounced back from that."*

✓ *"Anyone else would have folded, but I learned the game."*

✓ *"If I hadn't gone through that, I wouldn't be ten steps ahead today."*

- Now **your past isn't a weakness—it's proof you're untouchable.**

◉ Step 4: Make People Think Your Past Gives You an Edge Over Them

- The final move? **Turn the lesson into leverage.**

- If you were betrayed, **you now read people better than anyone else.**

- If you lost money, **you now know how to build it back smarter.**

- If you got outplayed, **you now see the game clearer than your competitors.**

- This **forces people to respect you—because your past gave you knowledge they don't have.**

Now here's the killer move—**once you've reframed your past, no one can ever use it against you again.** The moment they bring it up, **you look stronger, and they look desperate.**

Bottom line? You don't hide from your past—you turn it into proof that you're sharper, tougher, and impossible to kill. And when people see that? **They stop looking at your failures as losses… and start seeing them as the reason you're dangerous as fuck.**

Tactic 21.5:
Never Let Them See You Weaken

A damaged reputation doesn't destroy you—acting weak does.

People don't actually care about **right or wrong.** They care about **who looks like they're still in control.** The second you

act defensive, nervous, or desperate, people **assume the accusations are true.** But if you stand firm? If you **move like nothing phases you?** They **second-guess their doubts.**

Strength isn't about **having a perfect record**—it's about making people believe you **can't be taken down.** And if you master that? **No matter what happens, you stay on top.**

Here's how to **never let them see weakness—no matter what's thrown at you.**

Step 1: Control the First Impression–Calm, Unbothered, Unshaken

- The moment you react, people **judge your energy.** If you look **flustered, angry, or defensive,** they smell blood.

- Instead, **stay still, stay measured, stay bored.** If you look like you've **heard worse**, people assume the situation **isn't a big deal.**

  - *"Oh, this? Not even worth my time."*

  - *"People say dumb shit all the time. What else is new?"*

  - *[Smirk] "They're really trying, huh?"*

Step 2: Never Acknowledge That You're 'In Trouble'

- The more **you act like you're dealing with a crisis, the more people believe you have one.**

- **Never say you're fixing things, never act like you're 'recovering.'**

- Keep your schedule moving. Keep showing up where you belong. **Make it clear you haven't lost anything.**

  - *"Everything's business as usual."*

- *"People are always looking for a scandal—let them waste their time."*

- *"Anyway, let's talk about something that actually matters."*

Step 3: Let the Accuser Burn Themselves Out

- When you don't react, **they keep pushing harder.** That's exactly what you want.

- The more desperate they get, the **more unstable they look.**

  - If they're screaming while you're **calm**, people question **their credibility.**

  - If they **keep bringing it up** while you move forward, they look **obsessed.**

  - Eventually, **people get bored of their drama**—and you walk away untouched.

Step 4: Reassert Dominance Without Explaining Yourself

- When you **do** speak, it should be **a power move, not a defense.**

- **No explaining. No "I just want to clear things up." No justification.**

- Instead, you make **a single, sharp statement that shuts it down.**

  - *"People believe what they want. I don't waste time on that."*

  - *"If you need me, I'll be busy winning."*

  - *"I don't respond to nonsense—I let results speak."*

- Now, people **don't just stop questioning you—they see you as stronger than before.**

Final Power Move

Weak people **chase approval,** hoping to be "accepted" back into favor. **Strong people don't need validation.** They move **like nothing can touch them.** And when people see that? They **forget the attack ever happened—because you never let it become part of your story.**

Bottom line? You never **fight for your reputation.** You move like it was **never in question.** Because when people believe you **don't give a fuck?** They start to believe **there was never a reason to.**

> *Crisis doesn't reveal character—it reveals control. Panic exposes amateurs, silence crowns professionals. The ones who survive aren't innocent; they're disciplined. They keep their mouths shut, their faces calm, and their knives clean. You don't outrun exposure—you outlast it.*

Chapter Aftermath

You don't recover from a hit by flailing—you recover by turning your downfall into a fucking monument. Every tactic in this chapter wasn't about saving face—it was about **rebuilding your throne** while your enemies are still busy dancing on what they thought was your grave. While they're tweeting, posting, and plotting, you're sharpening your next move in silence, stacking leverage, and making damn sure they never get another shot.

This isn't redemption. It's retaliation with a velvet glove. You don't scream innocence—you bleed indifference. You let them throw dirt while you dig their reputational graves. Sympathy? Weaponized. Blame? Reassigned. Silence? Loaded. Comebacks? Engineered. You're not just surviving the scandal—you're **owning the aftermath like you scripted it from day one**.

You don't panic. You pivot. You don't explain. You erase. And when it's all said and done, you don't just walk away clean—you walk away **stronger, scarier, and more untouchable** than you were before the fallout even started. Because real power doesn't avoid damage—it turns damage into dominance.

CHAPTER NINE
The Psychology of Legacy

Power isn't about winning once—it's about never losing again. Most people treat power like a fucking trophy, like once they get it, they can sit back and enjoy the view. That's why they don't last. Power isn't a prize—it's a seat at a table where someone is always trying to pull the chair out from under you. You don't just need to win. You need to rig the whole goddamn game so that no matter what happens, you stay on top.

This chapter is about long-term dominance. How to stay relevant while others fade, control the future by twisting the present, and make sure any motherfucker who even thinks about rising against you gets shut down before they become a problem. You don't just want influence—you want to become permanent. And when you reach that level? No one can take you out. Not now. Not ever.

Lesson 22: Making Yourself Irreplaceable

Tactic 22.1
Why Power is a Long Game—Thinking 10 Moves Ahead

Most people play for **today**, and that's why they get **fucking crushed** tomorrow. Power isn't about **winning battles**—it's about **winning the war before anyone realizes it started.** The strongest players aren't reacting to what's happening now—they're **ten steps ahead**, setting traps, building leverage, and **shaping the future before anyone else gets a say.**

The dumbest thing you can do? **Get comfortable.** The second you think you've "made it," **someone is already planning your downfall.** That's why the real power moves aren't made **in the moment**—they're set in motion **months or years before the rest of the world catches up.** The people who win long-term **don't just think ahead—they make sure no one else can keep up.**

Here's how you stay **miles ahead of the competition while they're still playing checkers.**

- ◎ **Always Assume Someone is Plotting Against You**

    - Paranoia isn't a flaw—it's survival. **Someone, somewhere, wants what you have.**

    - The best way to stop a threat? **See it coming before it forms.**

    - Always ask yourself: *"Who benefits if I fail?"* Then **move first.**

- ◎ **Set Up Future Wins Before You Need Them**

    - **Most people only build leverage when they're in trouble.** That's too fucking late.

    - Make alliances, plant seeds, and set traps **long before you need them.**

    - By the time people realize you've stacked the deck, **the game's already over.**

- ◎ **Never Play Just One Move at a Time**

    - Power is **never** about what's happening **now**—it's about **what happens next.**

- Every move should have **at least three follow-ups** ready to go.

- If they counter your play, **make sure it only opens the door to your real plan.**

◉ **Make People Think They Have the Upper Hand**

- The best move? **Let them think they've won while they're walking into your trap.**

- The second they get comfortable, **you rip the floor out from under them.**

- Nobody fears a predictable player—**they fear the one they never see coming.**

Here's the **real difference** between winners and losers—**losers react, winners manipulate.** If you're playing the long game, you're **not waiting for power shifts—you're creating them.** You see the battlefield **before anyone else even knows there's a fight.**

Bottom line? If you're not thinking ten moves ahead, **you're already fucking losing.** And when the future arrives, you'll either be **the one in control** or **the idiot wondering how the hell it slipped away.**

Tactic 22.2:
The Immortal Influence—Staying Relevant Even After You Step Back

Power doesn't mean shit if people forget you the second you step away. **The weak think influence is about being in the spotlight—real players know it's about never being out of the conversation.** If you set things up right, you don't have to be **physically present** to still control the game. People will still **quote you, seek your approval, and fear crossing you,** even when you're nowhere to be seen.

Most people burn out because **they make power dependent on their presence.** The moment they leave, they become **irrelevant.** The key to staying untouchable is **building a presence so strong that even when you're not around, you're still in control.**

Here's how to make sure **you never fade, even after stepping back.**

◉ **Step 1: Make People Dependent on Your Influence**

- If people **can function without you,** they will. **Your job is to make sure they can't.**

- Create **systems, ideas, and structures that are so embedded in their world** that they can't escape them.

- Make people feel like **they need your insight, your approval, your methods—long after you've left.**

- *Example:* A business leader who trains employees to rely on **his system** ensures that, even when he retires, **his name still carries weight.**

◉ **Step 2: Leave Your Name in Every Room, Even When You're Not There**

- The best power move? **Make sure people still talk about you, even when you're gone.**

- Train **loyalists** to mention you strategically:

  ✓ *"This is exactly how [your name] would have done it."*

  ✓ *"You know who'd have the best take on this? [Your name]."*

  ✓ *"This situation reminds me of what [Your name] used to say."*

- When people keep **repeating your name,** they keep reinforcing your **power and influence—even when you're invisible.**

◉ **Step 3: Control Your Own Mythology**

- **People love legends.** Your job is to make sure they turn you into one.

- Instead of being known for a **single achievement**, make your story **bigger than reality.**

- Frame your past in ways that **make your name larger than life**:

  ✓ *"Back when I was running things, nobody made moves without checking with me first."*

  ✓ *"People don't know the half of what really went down back in the day."*

- If the **story sounds legendary, people will repeat it —even if it's exaggerated.**

◉ **Step 4: Only Make Strategic Appearances**

- If you want to **stay relevant**, don't be **too available.**

- The **less often people see you,** the more your presence **feels like an event.**

- Drop into key moments, make an impact, and then **fade out again** before people feel like you're always there.

- **Example:** A retired CEO who only speaks once a year at a major event **keeps his name alive** while still feeling exclusive.

Here's what separates **temporary power from lasting dominance —one is built on visibility, the other is built on influence.** If you have to be **constantly seen** to be relevant, you're playing **too small.** The real power move is making sure **you never fade, even when you step back.**

Bottom line? People should still be saying your name, quoting your words, and following your influence **years after you're gone.** And if you set things up right, **they'll still be wondering what move you're making next—even when you're not making any moves at all.**

> *Power doesn't last because you're smart —it lasts because no one can function without you. You don't build relevance; you build dependency, brick by fucking brick, until removing you feels like suicide. The goal isn't to be admired; it's to be necessary, to the point where even your enemies have to protect your name to protect themselves. When you've made yourself irreplaceable, you don't retire—you haunt the place forever.*

Lesson 23: Controlling the Future by Controlling the Present

Tactic 23.1:
The "Invisible Hand" Method—Long-Term Influence Without Being Seen

The biggest mistake people make? **They want to be seen as powerful.** They crave the spotlight, the recognition, the fucking ego boost. **And that's why they never last.** The second people know where the power is, **they start looking for ways to take it down.** The real game isn't about **being the king—it's about making sure the king can't move without you.**

That's the **Invisible Hand Method**—where you call the shots without anyone knowing you're running the whole goddamn show. You don't just **pull strings—you make sure no one even sees the strings exist.** By the time people figure out who's actually in control, **it's too late to stop you.**

Here's how you **own the game from the shadows.**

Step 1: Let Other People Take the Credit, But Keep the Control

- Power isn't about **getting credit**—it's about **making the decisions.**

- Give others the **title, the attention, the fucking pressure.** Let them **carry the weight while you stay untouchable.**

- *Example:* Instead of being the CEO, **be the "advisor" who actually makes the decisions.** The one everyone **checks in with before making a move.**

Step 2: Make People Think They're Acting on Their Own

- The best manipulation? **The kind where they don't even realize they're being manipulated.**

- Instead of telling people what to do, **plant the idea and let them think it was theirs.**

  ✓ *"You know what would be really smart?"*

  ✓ *"I wonder what would happen if someone took advantage of that opening…"*

  ✓ *"I bet the smart move would be to push this now."*

- If they think it's **their decision, they'll fight harder for it.** You don't need to push—**they'll push for you.**

Step 3: Control Information Flow–Never Give People the Full Picture

- **Information is power.** The second someone knows as much as you, **you become replaceable.**

- Only give people **what they need to act—never more.**

  ✓ Keep them **relying on you** for insight.

  ✓ If they start thinking they know everything, **introduce doubt to pull them back in.**

- *Example:* If you **control access to information,** you **control the outcome**—without anyone realizing you're the one setting the stage.

Step 4: Let Others Take the Heat While You Stay Clean

- Being the **obvious power** makes you a **target.** Make sure **someone else is always in the line of fire.**

- If a move backfires, **they take the hit—not you.**

  ✓ *"I was just giving my perspective; it was their call."*

  ✓ *"That wasn't my decision, but I see why they made it."*

  ✓ *"I thought it was risky, but hey, they went for it."*

- If something **goes well, you were involved. If it fails, you were never really part of it. That's how you stay untouchable.**

Final Power Move

The real power **isn't in being the leader—it's in being the one the leader can't function without.** The best players don't sit on the throne, **they build the fucking kingdom and decide who gets to wear the crown.**

Bottom line? If people know you're in control, **you're already vulnerable.** The second you learn to make moves **without leaving fingerprints,** you stop being a target. **You don't just win the game—you become the goddamn game master.**

Tactic 23.2:
Creating Systems That Keep You in Power Even When You're Gone

Power that depends on **you** isn't real power—it's a fucking job. If your influence **only lasts as long as you're around to enforce it,** then you don't have real control. The real game isn't about **holding power—it's about making sure it keeps working for you, even when you step away.**

The biggest mistake people make? **They make themselves too necessary.** They think being "indispensable" is strength. **It's not.** It's a goddamn liability. **If everything depends on you, it dies with you.** The real power move is **building a system that runs itself—one that enforces your will long after you've left the room.**

Here's how you set up **self-sustaining control** so your influence lasts—even when you're not around.

Step 1: Replace Personal Authority with Structural Control

- **If you have to personally make every decision, you're doing it wrong.**

- The key is to **build rules, policies, and structures that force people to act in your favor—without needing you to enforce them.**

- *Example:* A CEO who creates **a company culture that rewards loyalty to him personally** doesn't have to micromanage—his followers **self-police anyone who steps out of line.**

Step 2: Make People Dependent on Your System, Not Just You

- If people rely on **you**, they might eventually decide they don't need you anymore. **But if they rely on the system you built, they can never break away.**

- The trick? **Make sure the system you create always benefits those who follow it—and punishes those who don't.**

- *Example:* A politician who builds a network where **his people benefit as long as he's in the game** ensures they have a vested interest in keeping him relevant.

Step 3: Install Gatekeepers Who Enforce Your Rules for You

- You shouldn't have to **fight every battle yourself—** train **loyalists** to do it for you.

- **Give people just enough power that they feel important, but never enough to overthrow you.**

- *Example:* The best dictators don't rule alone—they create **a tier of enforcers who depend on them to stay in power.**

Step 4: Make It Impossible to Remove You Without Collapsing the System

- The final move? **Tie your power into the foundation of the system itself.**

- If removing you means **losing money, losing stability, or bringing chaos,** no one will ever try.

- *Example:* A business owner who builds **key relationships only he can maintain** ensures that if he steps away, **the whole operation is at risk.**

Final Power Move

If you've done this right, **you don't have to fight for power— your system does it for you.** Your influence isn't tied to your presence, **it's embedded into the very foundation of how things run.** People don't just respect you **while you're in the room—they fear what happens if you're not there.**

Bottom line? If your power disappears the moment you do, **you never had real power to begin with.** Build a system that keeps you at the center, and you don't just control the game—you **become the fucking game.**

Tactic 23.3:
The Art of Training Your Replacement (Who's Still Under Your Control)

Most people don't think about **who comes after them** until it's too late. That's why they either get **forced out** or leave behind **a mess that someone else takes over.** The real power move? **You don't just pick your replacement—you train them, shape them, and make sure they never truly outrank you.**

If you do this right, **your influence never dies** because the person taking your place is still **acting in your interests.** They think they're in charge, but **they're still following your playbook, using your strategies, and keeping your name alive.**

Here's how you create a **replacement who works for you— even when they think they don't.**

Step 1: Choose Someone Smart Enough to Run Things, But Not Smart Enough to Overthrow You

- The biggest mistake? **Training someone who doesn't need you.**

- You want them **capable enough to execute your vision, but never independent enough to challenge it.**

- Pick someone who **values your mentorship** and will always see you as the reason they got where they are.

Step 2: Make Sure They Adopt YOUR Playbook

- If they run things **their own way,** they could shift power away from you. **That can't happen.**

- While training them, **embed your strategies, your values, and your thinking.**

  ✓ Make them believe **your way is the only way.**

  ✓ Every time they succeed using your methods, **they reinforce their loyalty to you.**

- By the time they take over, **they're just an extension of you.**

Step 3: Keep Them Dependent on You

- You **never give them full control.** You always keep **one piece of the puzzle** to yourself.

- Maybe it's **key relationships only you manage.** Maybe it's **inside knowledge only you have.**

- The goal? **Make sure they always need you for something.** The second they realize they don't? **They're a threat.**

Step 4: Make Them Feel Like They Owe You Everything

- If they believe **you made them,** they won't challenge you.

- Remind them how **you gave them opportunities, showed them the ropes, taught them what no one else did.**

- The more they **tie their success to you,** the more they'll work to **keep your influence alive.**

Final Power Move

A true leader isn't the one **holding the title.** It's the one **who put the leader in place.** If you train your replacement **the right way,** you don't just walk away with power intact—you make sure **your influence never fades.**

Bottom line? If you leave and your name disappears, **you failed.** If you step back and people still follow your vision? **You didn't lose power—you just became a ghost in the machine.**

Tactic 23.4:
Building Self-Cleaning Power Structures—Eliminating Threats Before They Rise.

The biggest threat to your power? **The people who think they can replace you.** The second someone **starts believing they can take what you built,** they **will** try. The mistake weak leaders make? **They wait until the threat is obvious before dealing with it.** By then, **it's too late.**

The real move? **Set up a system where threats take themselves out before they ever become a problem.** If your structure is built right, **you don't have to kill competition—the system does it for you.**

Here's how you make sure **no one ever rises against you.**

Step 1: Make Advancement Depend on Loyalty to You

- If people can climb the ranks **without needing your approval, you're already vulnerable.**

- The path to power should **always go through you.** If they want to rise, **they have to prove loyalty first.**

- Anyone who **refuses to play by your rules?** They get blocked **before they ever gain traction.**

Step 2: Turn Potential Threats Against Each Other

- The easiest way to stop a rebellion? **Make sure the rebels never trust each other.**

- Create **competition** between ambitious people, so they spend **more time fighting each other than challenging you.**

- *Example:* Give two rising stars **just enough power** to feel important, but not enough to dominate. **Let them undermine each other while you sit back and watch.**

Step 3: Control the Watchdogs–Make Sure Someone is Always Watching for You

- You **should never be the one hunting for threats—** you should have **people who do it for you.**

- Build a network of **informants, enforcers, and gatekeepers** who will alert you **the second someone gets too ambitious.**

- *Example:* Smart leaders have **loyalists who keep an eye on rising talent**—and **neutralize problems before they get big.**

Step 4: Set Up Traps for the Disloyal

- You don't just **wait for someone to betray you**—you create situations that **expose disloyalty before it's dangerous.**

- Give a suspected threat **false information and see if it spreads.**

- Offer them **an opportunity that looks too good** and see if they take it behind your back.

- Once they **expose themselves,** they're done. **Gone before they even get started.**

Final Power Move

If you've built your system right, **you don't have to eliminate threats—they eliminate themselves.** The ambitious ones get stuck **fighting each other**, the disloyal ones **reveal themselves early**, and the ones who make it through? **They're too dependent on you to ever challenge your rule.**

Bottom line? If you have to personally stop a threat, **your system is weak.** Build it right, and no one even gets close. **By the time someone thinks about rising against you, they're already sinking.**

> *The future isn't a mystery—it's a hostage. You control it by rigging today so tightly that tomorrow has no choice but to obey. The weak adapt to what's coming; the strong design what's next and sell it as destiny. When every outcome leads back to you, you're not predicting the future—you're fucking authoring it.*

Lesson 24: The Final Evolution–Becoming Truly Untouchable

Tactic 24.1 :
The Power of Adaptability—Never Let Anyone Predict Your Next Move

The second people think they have you figured out, **you're already fucking dead.** Predictability is weakness. It gives enemies **a blueprint to take you down,** lets competitors **copy your moves,** and makes you **easy to replace.** The most dangerous person in any game? **The one no one can get a read on.**

The reason most people lose power? **They get too comfortable with what works.** They find a winning formula, **milk it dry, and die with it.** Meanwhile, the ones who stay on top **never stop evolving.** They know that survival **isn't about strength—it's about adaptability.**

Here's how you make sure **no one ever sees your next move coming.**

Step 1: Constantly Shift Your Tactics, But Never Your Core Power

- Weak people **switch strategies out of desperation.** Smart players **switch to stay ahead.**

- Your **core values and long-term game don't change—but your methods should always be fluid.**

- If you're known for being aggressive? **Go silent and let people wonder what you're up to.**

- If people expect you to be ruthless? **Show restraint—just long enough to lower their guard.**

Step 2: Never Let Anyone Get Too Comfortable Around You

- The second people **think they understand you,** they start planning against you. **Don't give them that chance.**

- Keep even your closest allies **guessing about what you'll do next.**

- Every now and then, **change the way you respond to situations—keep people unsure of how to approach you.**

- *Example:* One day, punish a mistake brutally. The next, **let a similar one slide. Watch the paranoia spread.**

Step 3: Keep Multiple Paths Open–Never Box Yourself In

- **The moment you rely on one strategy, you become easy to corner.** Always have **multiple ways out of a situation.**

- Never let an enemy force you into a position where **you only have one move left.**

- Build relationships **across different groups, different power circles.** If one collapses, **you're already tied into another.**

Step 4: Kill Expectations–Make Unpredictability Your Brand

- If people expect you to be one way, **flip the script.**

- If you're known for being cold, **be warm when it suits you.** If they think you're ruthless, **show patience— just long enough to catch them slipping.**

- Once unpredictability becomes **part of your identity,** no one will ever know when to strike. **That alone makes them hesitate.**

<u>Final Power Move</u>

If you do this right, **no one ever gets a clean shot at you.** They'll waste time **trying to figure you out,** while you stay **ten steps ahead.** The predictable players **get replaced, copied, or destroyed.** The adaptable ones? **They own the game forever.**

Bottom line? You either evolve, or you get left behind. **If they can predict you, they can plan against you. If they can't? You fucking own them**.

Tactic 24.2:
The "Controlled Chaos" Method—Keeping People Guessing

The worst thing you can be in any power game? **Predictable.** The second people know your patterns, they **plan around you, manipulate you, and eventually replace you.** That's why the smartest players don't just **adapt**—they create **chaos on purpose.** They make sure no one can ever pin them down, **never fully understand them, and never feel completely comfortable in their presence.**

Chaos isn't about **acting reckless**—it's about **strategic unpredictability.** The kind that keeps people **on edge, second-guessing themselves, never quite sure where they stand with you.** Because when they don't know what you'll do next, **they can't prepare for it.**

Here's how you **make unpredictability your most dangerous weapon.**

Step 1: Never React the Same Way Twice

- People **study behavior**—they look for **patterns, habits, triggers. Kill that immediately.**

- **One day, let something slide.** The next, **go nuclear over something small.**

- Make sure **people feel like they need to double-check their moves before they make them.**

- If people always know how you'll react, **they'll start playing you.** If they don't? **They tread carefully.**

Step 2: Switch Between Ruthlessness and Mercy

- **If you're always ruthless, people expect it.** If you're always forgiving, **they exploit it.**

- The trick? **Change it up—randomly, but deliberately.**

  - ✓ Someone screws up? **Let it go once.** The next time? **Bury them.**

  - ✓ When people think they understand your limits, **move them.**

  - ✓ The goal is to make sure **no one ever feels safe making assumptions about you.**

Step 3: Introduce Disruptions That Work in Your Favor

- People expect **stability—take it away.**

- Every now and then, **drop a piece of shocking information, make a move no one expected, shake things up just enough to throw people off their game.**

- If people feel like **anything could happen,** they become **hesitant, slower, easier to manipulate.**

- *Example:* If a rival thinks they're safe, **throw a wild card their way—just enough to make them nervous.**

Step 4: Keep Your Next Move a Mystery–Even to Your Closest People

- If **no one knows your full plan,** no one can stop it.

- When people ask about your next move, **keep it vague. Keep them wondering.**

- The less people **understand your endgame,** the more **control you have over how they react.**

Final Power Move

If you do this right, **people will always feel slightly on edge around you.** They won't know if you're about to **reward them or destroy them.** That hesitation? **That's control.** When people **fear the unknown,** they move **carefully, cautiously, and never against you.**

Bottom line? Predictability makes you a **target.** Unpredictability makes you **a fucking nightmare to deal with.** Keep people **guessing, second-guessing, and never fully prepared,** and you'll always **own the game.**

Tactic 24.3:
The Fear-Respect Balance—How to Command Both Without Losing Control

Power isn't about **just being feared or just being respected.** The real power play? **Balancing both so perfectly that people follow you out of admiration—but know damn well what happens if they step out of line.**

Most people screw this up. They either **go too soft and get walked all over** or **go too hard and make enemies they don't need.** But if you **master the balance?** You create an environment where people **want** to be on your side but **never even think** about crossing you.

Here's how you **command both fear and respect without ever losing control.**

Step 1: Make Sure Respect Comes First, But Fear is Always Present

- **People should admire you, but never feel too comfortable.**

- The second they think you're **only a "good guy,"** they start thinking **they can test you.**

- But if they only fear you? **They'll look for ways to bring you down.**

- The key is to build **respect through strength, competence, and results**—while making sure **there's always a shadow of fear beneath it.**

Step 2: Punish Loudly, Reward Quietly

- **Fear is built on examples.** People don't fear you because of what you *could* do—they fear you because of what they've *seen* you do.

- If someone **crosses a line,** make sure **everyone knows how that played out for them.**

- But when you reward loyalty? **Do it quietly.** Make sure people know **good things happen when they're on your side, but don't make it look easy.**

- The goal? **They should want your respect—but fear losing it even more.**

Step 3: Be Unpredictable Enough That No One Feels Safe Testing You

- If people **always** know what gets a reaction, they'll **play around the edges.**

- The solution? **Sometimes, let things slide. Other times, crush someone over something small.**

- Keep people **guessing**—make them wonder **how far is too far.** The uncertainty **keeps them in check.**

Step 4: Create an Environment Where Losing You is the Real Threat

- **The ultimate control move?** Make people fear **not having you around more than they fear pissing you off.**

- If they step out of line, they don't just get punished— **they lose access, protection, and opportunity.**

⊙ If walking away from you means **losing everything they've built,** they'll make damn sure to **stay in line.**

Final Power Move

If you've done this right, **people will respect you because they admire your strength—but fear you just enough that they never even think about crossing you.** They'll follow you because they **want to**—but they'll stay in line because they **have to.**

Bottom line? Fear alone makes enemies. **Respect alone makes you weak.** But if you get the balance right? **You don't just hold power—you make sure no one ever dares to take it from you.**

> *Adaptability isn't flexibility—it's weaponized chaos. You bend so you never break, shift so they never land a punch, and evolve faster than anyone can study your pattern. The ones who cling to identity become fossils, worshipped and forgotten in the same breath. The shapeshifter lives forever, because no one can kill what never stays still.*

Lesson 25: The Final Rule—Master the Game or Be Played

Tactic 25.1
Why Most People Will Never Win the Power Game

Most people **aren't built for this.** They think they are. They **like the idea of power,** of being the one in control. But when it comes down to it? **They fold.** They get emotional. They hesitate. They **crack under pressure and let the game eat them alive.**

Here's the truth—**power isn't fair, it isn't kind, and it sure as hell doesn't wait for weak people to figure it out.** The ones who win aren't necessarily **the smartest or the most talented.** They're the ones who **understand the rules and are willing to do what others won't.**

Here's why most people fail—and why you won't.

Step 1: They Think Power is About Being Liked

- Weak people **confuse influence with popularity.** They think if people like them, they'll stay in control. **Wrong.**

- Power isn't about being **liked**—it's about being **needed, respected, or feared.**

- The moment you chase approval instead of control, **you've already lost.**

Step 2: They Make Emotional Decisions

- Power is cold. **It doesn't give a fuck about feelings.**

- Most people get played because they **react instead of calculate.**

  ✓ Someone insults them? They lash out.

  ✓ They feel guilty? They backtrack.

  ✓ They get comfortable? They stop adapting.

- Emotions make you **predictable—and predictable people get eliminated.**

Step 3: They Wait for Permission Instead of Taking What's Theirs

- Power isn't **given**—it's taken. The ones who lose **wait for a perfect opportunity that never comes.**

- The winners? They **make the move, create the opening, force the situation in their favor.**

- If you hesitate, if you ask, if you wait for a sign? **Someone else is already making their move.**

Step 4: They Don't Have the Stomach for the Game

- Power requires **cutting people off, making hard choices, burning bridges when necessary.**

- Most people **flinch** when it's time to make those moves. They **rationalize, hesitate, or "give people one more chance."**

- The winners? **They do what's necessary, no hesitation, no second-guessing.**

Final Power Move

This game isn't for **the weak, the hesitant, or the ones looking for fairness.** If you're in, **be all the way in.** If you want control, **take it.** If you think someone else is going to **hand it to you,** do yourself a favor—**get the fuck out of the way.**

Bottom line? Most people fail because they **can't handle what power really takes.** If you don't have the stomach for it, **step aside.** Because the ones who do? **They don't just win—they own the whole goddamn board.**

Tactic 25.2 :
How to Spot the Next Threat Before It Arrives

The biggest threat **isn't the one coming at you—it's the one you don't see until it's too late.** Power doesn't get taken overnight. **It gets chipped away, little by little, by people who smile in your face while sharpening the knife behind your back.** The ones who stay on top? **They see the betrayal before it happens.**

Weak leaders wait until **they're under attack.** Smart ones **eliminate the threat before it even becomes a problem.** If you're reacting, **you've already lost.** If you're proactive, **they never even get a chance.**

Here's how you spot a snake before it bites.

Step 1: Watch for Sudden Ambition

- The quiet, loyal types? **They're fine—until they start looking too comfortable in your world.**

- If someone who used to be **content with their place suddenly wants "more,"** it's time to start paying attention.

- *Example:* The protégé who suddenly starts **building their own network, making moves without checking in, getting just a little too confident?** That's not growth. **That's a future problem.**

Step 2: Track Small Acts of Independence

- No one betrays you **all at once.** It starts with **small tests**—stepping outside your authority, making decisions without you, building their own influence.

- One time? **Maybe a mistake.** Twice? **That's a pattern.** Three times? **You're looking at a threat in the making.**

- They'll **always** downplay it—*"Oh, I just thought it was easier this way." "I didn't think you'd care."* **Bullshit.** They knew exactly what they were doing.

Step 3: Look for People Who Start Making Themselves Unreplaceable

- The smartest threats **don't challenge you directly— they embed themselves so deep into your system that you start depending on them.**

- The moment someone **makes themselves too critical to your operation,** they're positioning themselves to **either take over or hold leverage against you.**

- *Example:* The "loyal" advisor who starts **handling things only they understand, becoming the gatekeeper of key relationships, making sure you need them to function?** That's a problem.

Step 4: Test Their Loyalty Before They Think You're Watching

- Give them **a fake opportunity** and see if they take it without looping you in.

- Feed them **misleading information** and see if it comes back to you from someone else.

- If you think they might turn? **They already have.** Cut them loose before they get the chance.

Final Power Move

If you're surprised by betrayal, **you weren't paying attention.** The best defense isn't reacting fast—it's **not having to react at all.** The moment someone **thinks they have room to rise against you, you've already failed.**

Bottom line? Stay paranoid, stay ahead, and never let a threat breathe long enough to become real. The best way to deal with a snake? **Crush it before it learns how to bite.**

Tactic 25.3:
The Only Three Things That Actually Matter in Influence

Most people overcomplicate influence. **They think it's about charm, intelligence, networking, or some bullshit "leadership" skills.** It's not. Power doesn't care if you're **smart, likable, or even good at what you do.** You can be a fucking idiot, and if you master these three things, **you'll still control everything.**

If you strip influence down to its core, **only three things actually matter.** Master these, and you'll **own any room, any deal, and any person you set your sights on.**

1. Perception–Control What They See, and You Control What They Believe

- The truth is irrelevant. **Reality is whatever people think it is.**

- If you can shape how people see you, **you don't have to be powerful—you just have to look like you are.**

- People assume **confidence means competence, success means intelligence, and authority means legitimacy.**

  ✓ If you move like you belong, **no one questions it.**

  ✓ If you act like you're in control, **they follow.**

  ✓ If you let them see weakness, **you've already lost.**

2. Leverage–Make Sure Everyone Has Something to Lose

- People don't stay loyal because they like you. **They stay because it benefits them.**

- If someone can walk away from you without consequence, **you don't have influence—you have a temporary alliance.**

- The trick? **Make sure they have more to lose by leaving than by staying.**

  - ✓ Control **opportunities**—be the one who gives them access to things they can't get without you.

  - ✓ Control **information**—know things they don't want public.

  - ✓ Control **relationships**—make them feel like losing you means losing their place in the world.

- If they know **turning against you costs too much,** they'll never turn.

3. Scarcity–Make Them Feel Like They Can't Replace You

- **Influence dies the second people think you're replaceable.**

- You don't want them thinking, *"I'll find someone else."* You want them thinking, *"Without them, I'm fucked."*

- Be the **only person** who can provide what you provide, whether that's **insight, connections, access, or protection.**

- If they believe they **need you,** they'll tolerate anything to keep you happy.

Final Power Move

Master these three, and **you can walk into any room and take over.** Ignore them, and **you're just another face in the crowd.** Influence isn't about being **the best—it's about making sure people can't function without you.**

Bottom line? Control perception, own leverage, make yourself irreplaceable. If you do that, **you don't just have influence—you fucking own it.**

> *This isn't a sport—it's a blood economy where hesitation is bankruptcy. The players who flinch end up trophies on someone else's wall. Every rule, every system, every alliance exists to serve whoever's ruthless enough to rewrite it in real time. You either master the game, or you wake up one day realizing you've been the entertainment all along.*

Chapter Aftermath

Power isn't what you hold—it's what keeps holding even when you're gone. That's the difference between kings and legends: kings get remembered; legends *get obeyed*. This chapter wasn't about fame or glory—it was about **installing your name into the fucking infrastructure** so deeply that removing it would collapse the whole system. When every move, every rule, every leader still bleeds your blueprint? You didn't just win—you became permanent.

You didn't rise to dominate today—you rose to outlast tomorrow. While others fight for status, you engineered **self-sustaining control**: systems that defend you, enemies that neutralize themselves, successors who serve your interests even while thinking they're in charge. That's not influence—that's immortality with a kill switch.

Let the power-chasers burn out trying to go viral. Let the loud ones die on stages they built too fast. You're past that. You're the whisper behind every decision, the echo in every alliance, the blueprint they *can't* change without killing themselves in the process. That's legacy. That's fear wrapped in respect, hidden behind ritual.

Bottom line? If they can't erase you without erasing the game itself, you've already won. **That's not staying relevant—that's becoming a fucking religion.**

www.ingramcontent.com/pod-product-compliance
Lightning Source LLC
Chambersburg PA
CBHW070026100426
42740CB00013B/2604